Camera

Feminism, Culture, and Media Studies

The Place of the Contemporary Female Director
Special Issue Editors Therese Davis, Belinda Smaill, and Patricia White

Introduction: The Place of the Contemporary Female Director
Therese Davis and Belinda Smaill · 1

The Male Sojourner, the Female Director, and Popular European Cinema: The Worlds of Susanne Bier
Belinda Smaill · 5

The Minor Transnationalism of Queer Asian Cinema: Female Authorship and the Short Film Format
Olivia Khoo · 33

"Becoming-Girl" in the New Russian Cinema: Youth and Valeria Gai Germanika's Films and Television
Julia Vassilieva · 59

Between Worlds: Indigenous Identity and Difference in the Films of Darlene Johnson
Therese Davis · 81

The Kids Are All Right, the Pursuits of Happiness, and the Spaces Between
Jodi Brooks · 111

Beyond Indiewood: The Everyday Ethics of Nicole Holofcener
Claire Perkins · 137

Editors: Lalitha Gopalan, Lynne Joyrich, Homay King, Constance Penley, Tess Takahashi, Patricia White, and Sharon Willis

Advisory Editors: Paula Amad, Joanne Bernardi, Shohini Chaudhuri, Rey Chow, Wendy Hui Kyong Chun, Mary Desjardins, Mary Ann Doane, Rosa-Linda Fregoso, Bishnupriya Ghosh, Jennifer González, Elena Gorfinkel, Roger Hallas, Amelie Hastie, Jennifer Horne, Bliss Cua Lim, Ana López, Kathleen McHugh, Mandy Merck, Meaghan Morris, Frances Negrón-Muntaner, Kathleen Newman, Lisa Parks, B. Ruby Rich, Ella Shohat, Beretta Smith-Shomade, Jacqueline Stewart, and Sasha Torres

Managing Editor: Athena Tan

Editorial Assistants: Marcee Davis, Rachel Fabian, Hannah Goodwin, and Diana Pozo

Camera Obscura is published three times a year by Duke University Press, 905 W. Main St., Suite 18B, Durham, NC 27701.

Thanks to the University of California, Santa Barbara, for its support of the editorial office in the Department of Film and Media Studies. *Camera Obscura* also benefits from the generous support of the following institutions: Brown University, Bryn Mawr College, Swarthmore College, and the University of Rochester.

Thanks to the Department of Film and Media Studies at the University of California, Santa Barbara. The editors are also grateful to the College of Letters and Science for its generous support.

Send correspondence to *Camera Obscura*, Department of Film and Media Studies, University of California, Santa Barbara, CA 93106-4010.

Visit Duke University Press Journals at www.dukeupress.edu/journals.

Direct all orders to Duke University Press, Journals Customer Service, 905 W. Main St., Suite 18B, Durham, NC 27701. Volume 29 of *Camera Obscura* corresponds to issues 85–87. Annual subscription rates: print-plus-electronic institutions, $188; print-only institutions, $176; e-only institutions, $148; individuals, $30; students, $20. For information on subscriptions to the e-Duke Journals Scholarly Collections, see www.dukeupress.edu/library/eDuke.

Print subscriptions: add $11 postage and applicable HST (including 5% GST) for Canada; add $14 postage outside the US and Canada. Back volumes (institutions): $176. Single issues: institutions, $59; individuals, $12. For more information, contact Duke University Press Journals at 888-651-0122 (toll-free in the US and Canada) or 919-688-5134; subscriptions@dukeupress.edu.

Photocopies for course or research use that are supplied to the end user at no cost may be made without explicit permission or fee. Photocopies that are provided to the end user for a fee may not be made without payment of permission fees to Duke University Press. Address requests for permission to republish copyrighted material to Rights and Permissions Manager, permissions@dukeupress.edu.

Direct inquiries about advertising to Journals Advertising Coordinator, journals_advertising@dukeupress.edu.

Camera Obscura provides a forum for scholarship and debate on feminism, culture, and media studies. The journal encourages contributions in areas such as the conjunctions of gender, race, class, and sexuality with audiovisual culture; new histories and theories of film, television, video, and digital media; and politically engaged approaches to a range of media practices.

Contributor Information

Camera Obscura seeks substantial essays (approximately 6,500–9,000 words, including endnotes) that engage with current academic and popular debates in feminism, culture, and media studies. We encourage potential contributors to browse recent issues of the journal for examples of the types of scholarship we currently seek.

Camera Obscura is also interested in short pieces (750–2,500 words) on current media practices, practitioners, resources, events, or issues for the section "In Practice: Feminism/Culture/Media." The editors encourage authors to use the short format to experiment with form in a critical context. The section includes solicited contributions and open submissions, with the intention of enriching dialogue between feminist media scholarship and the practices—production, distribution, exhibition, organizing, curating, archiving, research, and so on—that sustain it.

Please submit one electronic copy (as a Microsoft Word e-mail attachment to cameraobscura@filmandmedia.ucsb.edu) of the manuscript with a cover letter. Manuscripts should be double-spaced and use endnotes. *Camera Obscura*'s documentation style follows *The Chicago Manual of Style*, 16th ed., chap. 14.

Camera Obscura, Department of Film and Media Studies, University of California, Santa Barbara, CA 93106-4010; fax: 805-893-8630; e-mail: cameraobscura@filmandmedia.ucsb.edu.

Camera Obscura is distributed by Ubiquity Distributors, 607 DeGraw St., Brooklyn, NY 11217; phone: 718-875-5491; fax: 718-875-8047.

Indexing and Abstract Listings
For a list of sources in which *Camera Obscura* is indexed and abstracted, see www.dukeupress.edu/cameraobscura.

© 2014 by *Camera Obscura*
ISSN 0270-5346

Introduction: The Place of the Contemporary Female Director

Therese Davis and Belinda Smaill

The essays in this special issue originated in a two-day international workshop we convened at Monash University, Melbourne, in November 2011. Titled "Between Worlds: The Place of the Female Director in Twenty-First-Century Film Cultures and Feminist Theory," the workshop was motivated by the renewed intellectual energy in recent feminist film theory around questions of women's filmmaking. Our group shared a particular sense of excitement about Patricia White's work on emerging industrial and textual crossovers between women's cinema and world cinema, so we were delighted when she accepted our invitation to give a public lecture in Melbourne on this topic and to lead the workshop in her role as Faculty of Arts Distinguished Visiting Professor.[1] In turn, we were invited to propose this special issue to *Camera Obscura* and then to work as coeditors.

We organized the workshop around a series of case studies and invited junior and more senior women scholars to submit papers that identified and analyzed key issues in the field. The workshop elaborated on these issues through concentrated discussion. The event was partly inspired by the possibility of identifying avenues for collaboration among women scholars from diverse disciplines in the humanities. We were particularly interested in how an institutional culture of collaboration might be enabled in our university and believed that the question of the female director offered a fruitful place to begin. Acknowledging the interdisciplinary and transnational legacy of the feminist film tradition in Australia, which includes the work of influential scholars such as Meaghan Morris, Lesley Stern, Laleen Jayamanne, Helen Grace, and Barbara Creed, we saw the forum as an avenue for a group of newer Australian women scholars to consider how their individual research interests might be brought to bear on a new set of questions and problems for women and film. Our discussion encompassed women's film practice in Europe, South America, Asia, Australia, and North America.

Contributors to this issue were asked to consider the workshop theme of "between worlds." Rather than imposing a unifying paradigm, this theme was intended as a cue for authors to consider how, given the mutable cultural terrain of the twenty-first century, the work of female directors might be negotiating different, perhaps even disjunctive, worlds. In-betweenness thus functions throughout the following essays as a critical prism through which individual authors consider the current industrial, theoretical, and cultural values that frame female directors and their work. It encompasses existential and temporal worlds; geopolitical formations such as regions and nations; cultural worlds such as first nations, settler cultures, and diasporas; and the industrial worlds of art cinema, world cinema, and national cinemas. The essays offer approaches that, in some cases, make explicit the worlds that particular female directors navigate through and, in other cases, leave them implicit in the analytical framing. The methodological breadth is clear, with each contribution framing its object of inquiry differently. Some broach aspects of the conventional director study, others the scope of regional filmmaking and national cinema and politics.

Taken together, the essays offer an innovative way to approach women's film practice in the twenty-first century. The contemporary landscape of cinema production and interpretation is providing new possibilities for defining the female director as an object of analysis. This is due not only to systemic changes in transnational pathways for production and distribution but also to the visibility of directors like Kathryn Bigelow, Sofia Coppola, Lucrecia Martel, and others. Building on these shifts, and attending to examples beyond these much-discussed auteurs, each contributor in this issue examines a director and the manner in which her practice is uniquely contemporary as it moves between different worlds, cinematic and cultural.

Note

1. A version of this public lecture has been published as Patricia White, "Global Flows of Women's Cinema: Nadine Labaki and Female Authorship," in *Media Authorship*, ed. Cynthia Chris and David A. Gerstner (London: Routledge, 2013), 212–28, and is incorporated into Patricia White, *Women's Cinema/World Cinema: Projecting Twenty-First-Century Feminisms* (Durham, NC: Duke University Press, forthcoming).

Figure 1. *After the Wedding* (*Efter brylluppet*, dir. Susanne Bier, Denmark, 2006)

The Male Sojourner, the Female Director, and Popular European Cinema: The Worlds of Susanne Bier

Belinda Smaill

Several perceptive contextualizing studies of female directors have recently moved beyond codified formulations of the auteur.[1] Instead of focusing narrowly on the expressive qualities of a director's oeuvre, much scholarship in contemporary feminist film studies is attuned to thematic and aesthetic questions and to the materiality of commerce and access. The female director study constitutes a crucial optic within the discipline, offering new appraisals of the relationship between women and cinema and the public sphere. This work is particularly valuable where previously neglected or emerging paradigms of transnational or nonanglophone cinema are concerned. In this essay I examine different dimensions of worldliness in the work of Susanne Bier, one of the most visible female directors working in the European and US film industries. In particular, I question what her status as a female director might add to a reading of her work's circulation in the contemporary global terrain of film festivals and criticism.

In a recent essay, Kathleen McHugh provides an instructive point of departure for considering women filmmakers and transnational paradigms, drawing on Virginia Woolf's proclamation: "As a woman I have no country; as a woman I want no country; as a woman my country is the whole world."[2] McHugh takes Woolf's "'whole world' insight" as a starting point to establish and critique women's "ontologically troubled relation to space" and their historical status relative to national, public, and private space.[3] For McHugh, the "problem of the world" also entails an opportunity to analyze the specificities of women's and feminist film production (113). It acknowledges historical marginalization while bringing with it the potential for thinking beyond the nation. Describing the transnational as a way to further explore the legacy of women's relation to space, McHugh distinguishes this term from the homogenizing impulse of the global. Building on the work of Ella Shohat, she considers a transnational cohort of women filmmakers born between 1945 and 1960. This historical frame, for McHugh, brings into focus a generation influenced by feminism as well as by a cultural imaginary of globalization. This generation has moved beyond the primacy of national belonging in the postwar era while registering a shift in the meaning and category of "woman" that has accompanied the rise of transnational feminisms (120–21). The filmmakers McHugh includes in this categorization frequently offer transnational themes in their films and work within production regimes that are at least in part transnational. Moreover, the popular and critical reception of their work has been informed by feminism or framed by gendered taxonomies of genre classification.

A newer generation of women filmmakers, who are only now establishing reputations and significant bodies of work, falls outside the scope of McHugh's account. These filmmakers have emerged into different cultures of both film and feminism. Since approximately 1990, changes in the industrial landscape of European and anglophone cinema production have further decentered the paradigm of national cinema and affected the ways in which directors are discursively framed. Thomas Elsaesser observes:

"The traditional line between national and international, as well as between art cinema and commercial cinema, is no longer as clear-cut as it was during the confrontation between Europe and Hollywood between 1945 and roughly 1990."[4] He is insightful in his elaboration of this shift, so I quote him at length:

Co-productions have become the norm, rather than the exception, and contemporary auteurs feel neither called upon to be "artists" nor play the role of nationally representative figureheads. If for audiences the provenance of a film has diminished in importance as a reception category, insofar as directors are rarely judged by how well they fit into a predefined national cinema, the director auteur is still a relevant production category. S/he now functions within a different set of determinants than those encompassed by either national cinema or unique stylistic cinema. Rather, what matters now is how well local/national provenance can communicate with global/transnational audiences. (491)

If the altered transnational terrain that has become apparent over the last two decades has increasingly blurred boundaries within categories of production and reception, popular conceptions of feminism have also entered a new paradigm.

McHugh looks at the transnational cohort of female directors that emerged in the postwar period and began working between the mid-1960s and early 1980s. Postwar transnationalism, within this frame, coincided with second-wave feminism in a way that politicized and connected women globally and offered opportunities and resources not limited to national industries and institutions. I am interested in the conditions that enabled the generation of women filmmakers who were born in and after 1960, following this earlier transnational cohort. I suggest that there is a new environment for female labor and a changed discursive context for reading the female director and her work that concerns women like Bier who began their careers around or after 1990. In addition to the shifts observed by Elsaesser, the last two decades have been characterized by increasingly fluid avenues for distribution, given the advent of digital technologies and platforms such as the Internet. Not only are cinema formations changing but there is also a growing retreat from feminist politics in popular culture and a return to narrow feminine typologies with the postfeminist turn. Alongside these developments, a growing number of female artists and cultural producers opt not to align themselves with gendered politics and themes.[5] This new phase requires attention to how cinema production and reception categories influence the ways in which director brands and images are structured and signified alongside specific films.

Bier, born in 1960, is on the cusp of McHugh's cohort and offers a rich and important example of how a newer generation of female directors might be negotiating this recent terrain, not least because of her significant commercial success and visibility. Her sizable and consistent oeuvre lends itself to auteurist models of interpretation. Yet despite this and the small number of women of comparable status, there has been little scholarly discussion of Bier's cinema. Many female filmmakers begin their careers in documentary production or by directing television drama, and a large number remain in television production as a way to subsidize careers in feature film directing.[6] Bier took neither path and instead moved into the industry, directing predominantly features. Having directed fifteen feature films at the time of writing—including one made for television—Bier has an extensive oeuvre that can be broadly delineated as comedy during the 1990s and drama in the 2000s. The hinge for this shift is her contribution to the Dogme 95 movement, *Open Hearts* (*Elsker dig for evigt*, Denmark, 2002).

Bier's career and films emerge distinctively out of a Danish national cinema context while also showing strong transnational entanglements. Bier studied comparative religion and set design at the Bezalel Academy of Arts and Design in Jerusalem and architecture in London before enrolling in the National Film School of Denmark to study directing. She graduated in 1987. Her early films (those made between 1990 and 2000) are largely Swedish-language coproductions, including *Freud's Leaving Home* (*Freud flyttar hemifrån*, 1991), *Family Matters* (*Det bli'r i familien*, 1994), *Like It Never Was Before* (*Pensionat Oskar*, 1995), and *Once in a Lifetime* (*Livet är en schlager*, 2000). In the 1990s she preferred dark family comedies. Her Danish romantic comedy *The One and Only* (*Den eneste ene*, 1999) was the most commercially successful film in Danish cinema history at the time of its release. Yet Bier's transnational education and the cross-border nature of her early film work clearly show that factors outside the Danish national context have enabled her work. Indeed, her productions in the 1990s index a broader institutional movement toward a Nordic cinema formation. Over the last two decades, this regional top-down strategy has worked to emphasize coproductions and denationalize expressive markers in Scandinavian films.[7] Scandinavian financing agreements that have strategically privileged a regional, transnational sensibility over a national cinema sensibility offer a specific manifestation of Elsaesser's observation.

Bier's position within the postwar Jewish diaspora also references the effects of cross-border movements and twentieth-century geopolitical upheavals and distinguishes her within transnational Nordic cinema. Bier's father fled Nazi Germany to arrive in Denmark in 1933, while her mother's family escaped a Russian pogrom.[8] Critics and interviewers consistently note this family history. In a 2001 interview with Mette Hjort, Bier refers to this legacy: "I would love to make a film with a Jewish theme again at some point. It's clear that I know that world concretely and can easily describe it as a result. . . . I do think that I, as a modern Dane, at times end up feeling fairly alienated from typically Danish ways of relating to other people, particularly when it comes to family."[9] She has also noted, in reference to *Open Hearts*—which was made in the wake of the events of 11 September 2001—that the film was driven by a sense of fragility: "The screenwriter, Anders Thomas Jensen, and I actually met through my own very strong personal sense of potential catastrophe. I think this has to do with being Jewish and having a sense of history where the impossible is a possibility."[10] Bier's films consistently focus on the psychodynamics of family, whether for comedic or dramatic ends, and her statements in these interviews link this thematic interest to her second-generation migrant background. Her first feature, *Freud's Leaving Home*, places the Jewish family, dispersed across national borders and grappling with the legacy of the Holocaust, at the forefront of the plot. Bier's more recent films, *Brothers* (*Brødre*, 2004), *After the*

Wedding (*Efter bryluppet*, 2006), and *In a Better World* (*Hævnen*, 2010), thematize global mobility from a Danish perspective. Her 2012 film *Love Is All You Need* (*Den skaldede frisør*) returns to the comedy genre while remaining decisively transnational with an international cast, trans-European funding and shooting locations, and a multilingual script.

I recast McHugh's "problem of the world" to examine two ways in which Bier's films engage with gendered worldly spaces. The first part of this essay attends to the increasingly transnational dimensions of women's film practice to assess the critical and industrial terrain that shapes the reception and production of Bier's work as popular European cinema. This reception has frequently entailed divergent and arguably gendered estimations of her films' critical and cultural worth. Exploring a different dimension of the contemporary global public sphere, I go on to consider the worlds produced in *Brothers*, *After the Wedding*, and *In a Better World*. In all cases the film worlds focus on the intimacy of the Danish nuclear family while also developing distinctly transnational plotlines centered on the figure of the male sojourner. Both analytical frameworks are crucially concerned with how Bier's films address a popular audience within and across national borders, and what is at stake in this address for rethinking the figure of the female director.

The World of Bier's Popular European Cinema

In her interview with Bier, Hjort asks: "Do you think of yourself as a popular director?" Bier responds:

> I think that popular film, in a positive sense, is the ultimate goal. I do, of course, have a positive, inclusive sense of "popular" in mind here. I don't think that one should talk down to people, although this really happens a lot. However, if you have something to say and can express it with such precision and simplicity that it moves a lot of people, then I think you've achieved something important, especially in the case of film, for film is, after all, a popular medium. . . . I think of film as a type of mass communication and I care about reaching a lot of people, or particular kinds of people.[11]

Bier's statement describes popular cinema as maximizing its appeal to and cultural resonance for a given constituency of viewers. While her work makes the most of its audience base, as its commercial success in local and international markets suggests, it is not comprehensively categorized as popular cinema. Bier's films, their critical reception, and her director's statements frequently indicate a position between the worlds of art cinema and popular cinema. Close attention to her recent films reveals distinct markers of art cinema. Since the highly acclaimed *Open Hearts*, her films have revolved around Dogme-style handheld camerawork, location shooting, little or no artificial lighting, and minimal postproduction music. In *Open Hearts*, *Brothers*, and *After the Wedding*, the images' stark quality is heightened by the emphasis on character interactions through close-ups and medium shots. This visual style, coupled with the story lines' engagement with psychological questions, satisfies the taste economies of the market and arthouse audiences.

Louise Kidde Sauntved compares Bier's status as a director with that of art cinema auteur and compatriot Lars von Trier:

Bier has traveled the festival circuit extensively with her four most recent films, and has brought a lot of attention to the Danish film scene, though not as much as her countryman Lars von Trier, who has always overshadowed her internationally. Critics and festival programmers tend to find her work "too commercial" or "insufficiently artistic" by comparison. Last year *In a Better World* was turned down by Cannes, whereas von Trier is almost guaranteed a slot with each new film.[12]

Kidde Sauntved makes explicit reference to the festival infrastructure that bestows aesthetic and cultural legitimacy on arthouse production. These different statements acknowledge the art cinema associations that frame Bier's style and industrial context while also judging her work unsuccessful within this classification. Von Trier's cinema is not only deemed sufficiently artistic, it operates alongside his directorial brand to achieve the ideals of masculine, modernist auteurism. Alternatively, Bier's own director's statements and positive appraisals of her films favorably position her oeuvre as popular cinema.

For Richard Dyer and Ginette Vincendeau, the term *popular* brings with it a "productive messiness."[13] In part, this confusion emerges with the shorthand deployment of "popular" as synonymous with "commercial," "entertainment," "mainstream," "genre," and even "Hollywood." Yet Victor Perkins explains that popular cinema attends to audience understandings acquired through the specificity of everyday life: "The terms of access unite the formal with the cultural since what is learned in the ordinary processes of life varies with place and time."[14] By way of illustration, he notes that a French film may be accessible to a mass audience when released in France, but a subtitled version will cater to the niche structures of art cinema in the UK. Acknowledging how she considers the audience when constructing characters and situations, Bier notes: "There are a lot of people, who don't happen to live where we live or eat the kind of food that we eat, who simply won't get the point."[15] Her concern with transcending cultural specificities so that these audiences do "get the point" enables her to reach not only a regional, transnational audience but also a global one. Since 2002, Bier's films have achieved this global circulation. However, the dual markers of *arthouse* and *popular* have led to divergent perceptions of her cinema as largely mainstream in a local European context and as European arthouse cinema in English-speaking cultures.

In English-language film studies and criticism, the term *popular* is usually aligned with Hollywood and figured in opposition to European cinema. As Dimitris Eleftheriotis writes, "On the level of film theory, the conceptual categories of film studies do not take into consideration the popular European."[16] There are compelling reasons for exploring the classification and mobility of Bier's work through the messy prism of European popular cinema. The very messiness of this nomenclature offers an opportunity to investigate the different conditions for the circulation of her work.

Critics and reviewers have not reached consensus on the aesthetic value of Bier's style. In her review of *After the Wedding*, Manohla Dargis states that the film "opts for a style that might be called Dogme-lite, which mimics the movement's visual tropes but eschews its ethos and formal rigor to create what is, at core, canned realism."[17] Similarly, reviewer David Fear refers to *In a Better World* as "Haneke lite."[18] These characterizations position Bier's work in the US market as an inadequate art cinema when measured against the criteria of Dogme or Michael Haneke's acclaimed trans-European art cinema. The films are deemed unsuccessful when perceived solely as art cinema, but they fare much better as European popular cinema that seeks to resonate across borders. On the latter terms, the films are more persuasively understood as genre films that draw on familiar codes to amplify audience identification and that cross cultural boundaries with relative ease. As I have noted, Bier's early films focused on familial relationships and the domestic comedy. Arguably, the director's work since 2002 still works within genre, combining the Dogme style with melodrama.

While the Dogme rules eschew both genre and nondiegetic music, Bier's more recent films such as *After the Wedding* use minimal music and replicate the high emotionalism of melodrama. They produce oppressive melodramatic dilemmas through the orchestration of story and character rather than turning to *melos* to heighten emotion. Since these films adhere to the Dogme requirement of exclusively natural lighting, their domestic interiors often take on subdued or flattened tones that enhance the sense of televisual melodrama and the quotidian. In these films the male characters are at the center of the web of human relationships. They navigate narratives punctuated by weddings, funerals, marriage breakdowns, and the tribulations of the nuclear family. In particular, the films explore how men grapple with the pressure and desire to maintain their roles within conventional patriarchal domestic structures. Their undertakings in this arena are sabotaged constantly by forces beyond the characters' control. For example, children exacerbate a failing marriage by rebelling and instigating acts of violence (*In a Better World*), or a dying man's plans force the protagonist to confront a daughter he never knew existed (*After the Wedding*). It is men who undergo the most extreme challenges and emotional transformations in Bier's films, securing the status of these films as male melodramas.

The popular standing of Bier's work is reinforced by her connections with Hollywood. Bier has received two Academy

Award nominations for Best Foreign Language Film and won in that category for *In a Better World*. She made her directorial debut in Hollywood in 2007 with *Things We Lost in the Fire*. Additionally, *Brothers* was remade in the US and released in 2009, starring Tobey Maguire, Natalie Portman, and Jake Gyllenhaal, and a remake of *After the Wedding* is currently in production. While Bier's work translates well into Hollywood expectations and codes, her filmmaking does not operate on the same popular terms as Hollywood cinema does. In this respect, Meryl Shriver-Rice makes an important distinction between Bier's *Brothers* and the remake set in the US: "Like her Dogme work, Bier's *Brothers* is 'non-nationalist' in that it favors a global audience over an emphasis on Danish local culture and inclusion. However, when viewed in contrast with its Hollywood remake of the same title, Bier's film stands out as undeniably Nordic in its intimate psychological storyline and art-film aesthetics, while the Hollywood version manifests its own set of amplified national themes."[19] Significantly, this comment exemplifies how the categorization of art cinema and popular cinema is not fixed but rather relies on a dynamic between transnational and national that is influenced by the terms of production, popular reception, and criticism. Elsaesser's estimation that the success of a film is marked by how well local concerns can be harnessed to communicate with global audiences maps accurately onto Bier's achievements with a film such as *Brothers* and the global accessibility and appeal of a distinctively Nordic cinema. *Brothers*, as Shriver-Rice notes, offers a Nordic style of "psychological realism" (10). While in *Brothers* this style signals local specificity, it also translates into locations, characters, and plotlines that are meaningful for a global audience. Bier's film work differs from the various modes of Hollywood transnational cinema, which make nationally specific themes familiar to a global audience through Hollywood's historical dominance and market reach. An assessment of Bier's cinema and its reception must negotiate shifting markers of distinction. In many respects, this is because it has emerged from a specific historical-industrial context that determines the material conditions for directors, who must work in a terrain that has undergone significant transformation over the last two decades. This is especially complex for female filmmakers, as Bier's case demonstrates.

A series of slippages occur where Bier is concerned. First, entrenched—often anglophone—perceptions of European cinema commingle with Bier's films' increasingly transnational address and contribute to the uneven critical reception of her European work as inadequate art cinema. Second, the terms on which her films are negatively assessed frame the popular dimensions of the work pejoratively as feminine. The import of this extends beyond Bier to the historical devaluation of women's production through a conflation with negatively feminized discourses, including genre and emotion.

Bier's directorial image and her films sit in an indeterminate zone. Her films are most favorably assessed when they are understood as popular cultural artifacts rather than high art. In this context, they are appraised as offering "emotionally powerful drama."[20] They are vehicles for consistently strong performances from Scandinavian actors and convey what Kidde Sauntved calls "kitchen sink realism."[21] These appraisals are consistent with the large audiences the films attract and the crossover appeal or global currency of Bier's work. Negative assessments of her films describe the same qualities in disparaging ways. Reviewers have characterized her recent work as "apparent and schematic" and overly emotionalized, with "soap-operatic background noise and back-patting platitudes."[22] David Edelstein describes *In a Better World* as "an Oprah movie."[23]

A number of Anglo-American critics tend to measure Bier negatively against the modernist criteria of art cinema that is signified by its Europeanness. The term *soap opera* and the invocation of Oprah conflate the work with a devalued mass culture. The result, I argue, is an implicit feminization of both the film narratives and the director's brand. Negative evaluations of Bier's work seem to suppose that popular, mass cultural elements and art cinema modernism or realism cannot successfully coexist in a single film or oeuvre, or even film tradition.

Within the post-1990 transnational nexus of interpretation,

Bier is successful when classified in relation to popular European cinema and negatively gendered as a female director when evaluated against the imposed criteria of (European) art cinema modernism. In the next section I explore how the figure of the female director can be reconciled with that of a male character who is entangled in themes of ethical crisis and cosmopolitanism—high modernist qualities—in films that embrace the generic codes and elaborate emotional worlds of melodrama.

The World of the Male Sojourner in *Brothers, After the Wedding,* and *In a Better World*

Brothers, After the Wedding, and *In a Better World* were directed by Bier and written in collaboration with Anders Thomas Jensen. The three films explore recurrent themes and narratives, signaling a growing authorial interest in humanitarian issues and practices. For this reason, I pose them here as a trilogy. I wish to consider how transnationalism and genre are enacted in these films and how this might bear on questions of gender representation and women's film practice more broadly. While the previous section explored Bier's own oeuvre in light of the interpretive realm in which films and directors circulate, I now examine how the films depict social worlds through the deployment of plot, character, and style.

Although her work has at times been implicitly framed as feminized popular cinema or unworthy art cinema, Bier's trilogy is not specifically directed at a female audience, nor does it privilege female protagonists. Instead, the films that make up the trilogy focus on masculinity and dilemmas facing male culture and sociality. This interest in male-centered plots enhances the commercial currency of the films—female leads are less successful at the box office than male protagonists.[24] Yet *Brothers, After the Wedding,* and *In a Better World* all draw on the codes of melodrama to emphasize the ways in which the complex backdrop of war, globalization, and politics supplement and compel family dynamics. The figure of the male sojourner, the hero who must grapple with hefty humanitarian problems on the global stage, is made vulnerable by Bier as she exposes him to the labored and quotidian relations between lovers, husbands and wives, siblings, and children and parents. The trilogy thus reframes the modernist hero of art cinema through its embrace of melodrama, the prosaic, and the everyday.

In *Brothers*, the two siblings referred to in the title express masculinities posed in contradistinction. Michael (Ulrich Thomsen) is a military officer with a wife and two young children. At the outset of the film he and his unit are sent on a UN peacekeeping mission to Afghanistan. His younger brother, Jannick (Nikolaj Lie Kaas), is a moody reprobate who is cast in contrast to his brother's good character. When Michael is thought to have died in a helicopter crash, Jannick surprises the family and steps in to support his sister-in-law and her children. It is soon revealed that unidentified Afghan captors, presumably the Taliban, are holding Michael and that he is very much alive. While held captive, Michael is forced to kill a fellow soldier or face death himself. He eventually returns to his family psychologically altered. Suspicious of his brother's new role in his family, he is paranoid and violent.

In contrast, *After the Wedding* follows a single protagonist, Jacob (Mads Mikkelsen), who works at an orphanage in India. He returns unwillingly to his native Denmark at the request of a businessman he has never met, Jørgen (Rolf Lassgård), who plans to donate a large sum of money to the orphanage. Required to attend the wedding of Jørgen's daughter, Anna (Stine Fischer Christensen), Jacob realizes he is Anna's father. His relationship with Anna's mother, Helene (Sidse Babett Knudsen), now married to Jørgen, ended years ago due to the chaotic and adulterous lifestyle he led in India at the time. It soon becomes clear that Jørgen, a very wealthy, successful businessman, has a terminal illness and has decided to enlist a surrogate to take care of his family once he is gone. Although Jacob is eager to return to India—his home and the country where he sees his life's work taking place—he becomes bound to fulfill Jørgen's plan.

In a Better World's Danish title (*Hævnen*) means "the revenge," and it is revenge that offers the key motivation for the confrontations that are repeated through the plot. Early in the film two twelve-year-old boys meet and become friends in a small town in Denmark. They become close after one, Elias (Markus Rygaard), is bullied at school and the other, Christian (William Jøhnk Juel Nielsen), rescues him by attacking the tormentor with a bicycle pump and threatening him with a knife. Their relationship continues to evolve around the terms of violence and revenge, culminating in the bomb attack on the car of a man—an adult bully—who has harassed Elias's father, Anton (Mikael Persbrandt). In a parallel thread, Anton travels periodically to a refugee camp in an unnamed African nation to work as a doctor. In this context he is confronted with extreme violence against women, the victims of one particular warlord. Anton makes the decision to treat this man when he comes into the camp with a leg wound. However, after the warlord shows contempt for his victims, Anton loses his temper and expels him from the clinic, leaving him to be murdered by the local people.

In all of the films, husbands and fathers are placed in positions of crisis. They either kill, are killed, or face death directly. Bier explores the limits of and demands on the masculine psyche in these situations and how they play out in relations between individuals. These limits are staged most acutely in relation to a geographical elsewhere: the non-West or the global South. The impact of these other (or "othered") places and cultures reverberates in each narrative, magnifying protagonists' moral decisions and actions. These places provide faraway locales for the extremes of violence or altruism that inform the consciousness of the characters when they return to their native Denmark. In Danish suburbia they face a different set of quandaries—the quotidian pressures of the domestic realm and intimate relationships.

Leaving aside their generic status as melodramas, there is no overt or essential quality to these films that proclaims a female authorial stamp. Bier offers ambivalent statements about her identification with feminism and issues facing women. Referring to herself and two other Danish female directors, Lotte Svendsen and Lone Scherfig, Bier states: "We've broken with old style feminism. The women who were making films fifteen years ago were very interested in their being women. We're not."[25] This indicates neither a complete rejection nor an embrace of feminism. Nevertheless, the narratives of Bier's trilogy do draw attention to the problematic of Western masculinity and, at times, familial patriarchy through the figure of the Danish male sojourner.

This male figure appears in slightly different ways in each film. In *Brothers*, the relationship between the two brothers is explored in the film's predominant setting, Danish suburbia, and is the hinge on which two alternative masculinities are elaborated. The opening scenes of the film establish Jannick as consistently antagonistic and volatile. Michael, in contrast, is rendered as calm, authoritative, and above all responsible. The viewer's first impressions of their relationship are gleaned from a scene showing Michael meeting Jannick on his release from prison following a sentence for robbery and assault. In the close quarters of the car on the way home, the handheld camera moves between the two characters as Michael reveals that he has met with the female bank teller Jannick assaulted in the robbery. He urges his brother to visit her and apologize for his wrongdoing. The two begin to argue. The car screeches to a stop as Jannick pulls the hand brake and storms off across a sports field alone and on foot. After Michael is reported dead in Afghanistan, Jannick's transition into the responsible placeholder for Michael in the patriarchal family structure is gradual but clear, offering the character a distinct evolution within the narrative arc. This transition manifests as a substitution of types as Michael, clearly altered after his experiences in Afghanistan, descends into a sullen, erratic, and aggressive state upon his return.

While Jørgen in *After the Wedding* is seeking to secure a new patriarch for his family, it is Jacob who is tasked with the most difficult decision about good conduct, family, and charity. Jacob works in India at the outset of the film, and the country is clearly rendered as his emotional and physical home. The film follows his movement from the periphery to the European center (and then briefly back at the film's close). The orphanage where he works and the welfare of the boys there are his first consideration when he is asked to go to Denmark to meet the anonymous philanthropist. In Jacob's case, decisions about his responsibilities are tied to the attachments

Figure 2. *In a Better World* (*Hævnen*, dir. Susanne Bier, Denmark, 2010)

and deeds that require him to move between countries. The first adjustment he must make is to return to Denmark when he would rather stay in India. The second occurs when he chooses to stay in Denmark and accept responsibility for the nuclear family that waits for him, forgoing his pledge to the orphaned children. Jacob, of all the protagonists in Bier's trilogy, stands out as the one most attached to his residence away from Denmark. Even so, Jacob is able to disinvest in his alternative and peripheral home and make his life in Denmark, privileging his family there. The film, however, implies that the price of consolidating the patriarchal nuclear family may be too high.

Again beginning in an environment far from Europe, *In a Better World* positions Anton immediately against the chaotic and impoverished conditions of the African refugee camp where he works. During the course of the narrative, he travels there three times. Anton's past aligns him more with Jacob than with Michael: he is separated from his wife, Marianne (Trine Dyrholm), and in one conversation they discuss his past infidelity, the cause of the separation. When another man bullies Anton as his two sons and Christian look on, he attempts to defuse the situation without resorting to violence. His response suggests he is alert to the role he must play as masculine exemplar to the two boys. The question of proper conduct is addressed again in the refugee camp in a later scene, but in a way that offers a much more nebulous distinction between the ethical path and the unethical one. The warlord, the "Big Man" who is attacking women in the local population, is the second aggressor Anton must deal with, but this time in the parallel world of the camp. Although this man has committed irredeemable acts of violence, Anton agrees to save his infected leg, thus choosing between his Hippocratic oath and the wishes of the victims. Although the boys, Christian and Elias, are equally central as protagonists in the film, Anton's actions and decisions are the vehicle for the allegorical structure of the story. The scene in which he decides to throw the Big Man to the mob offers a conclusive moment in the narrative.

The elsewhere in the films is represented in ways that circumvent possibilities for realizing the specificity of location and historical context. Instead, the scenes outside Europe are platforms for universalizing human behaviors, particularly those concerning intersubjective ethical conduct. In *Brothers*, *After the Wedding*, and *In a Better World*, male characters struggle with the best ways to act within the nuclear family and how to model (masculine) conduct in relation to a range of other subjects, including soldiers, children, and refugees—the orphans that Jacob cares for in India, for example, or the patients Anton treats in the refugee camp in Africa. Michel Foucault has described ethics through a notion of selfhood and conduct and as a question of governmentality: "the government of the self by oneself in its articulation with relations with others."[26] Foucault's formulation is apposite for elaborating on the characterization of the male sojourner because it takes on questions of conduct and understands them in relation to behavioral rules and the production of modern subjectivities more broadly. Ethical conduct concerns "the relationship of the self to itself, and . . . the range of practices that constitute, define, organize, and instrumentalize the strategies that individuals in their freedom can use in dealing with each other" (xvii). In each film, albeit in different ways, the male protagonist experiences confusion and a lack of certitude in his endeavors to engage with others.

When these individuals venture out, traveling south to zones of poverty and war, the question of conduct can be further specified as an ethical cosmopolitanism, particularly in *After the Wedding* and *In a Better World*. A term that addresses the symptoms of increasing mobility in modernity, *cosmopolitanism* often refers both to an openness to other cultures within a given public sphere—an outward-looking imaginary—and to the experience of being exposed to cultures in ways that extend beyond everyday experience. Nikos Papastergiadis notes that cosmopolitanism "includes both a way of being in the world that entails a universalist aspiration for moral connectedness and an emergent social order that extends political rights beyond exclusivist territorial boundaries."[27] Cosmopolitanism characterizes an ethics of selfhood that is posed in relation to globalization and encounters with cultural otherness. The emphasis on masculine roles and dilemmas about responsible action throws Bier's characters and plots firmly into the realm of allegory and contributes to the popular address of the director's work. An address to a mass audience is more easily facilitated by recourse to allegory, which heightens familiar tropes and themes.

In some respects, acknowledging the allegorical qualities of Bier's trilogy could be a response to critics' characterizations of her work as schematic. Character typing enables a clear rendering of ethical conduct. For example, Michael is cast as the impeccable military officer and father who is forced into a moral transgression that transforms him. Anton is the somber doctor who is pushed to betray his professional code. There is a veneer of character complexity offered in the subplot of *In a Better World* that explores the effects of an affair on Anton's marriage, but this cannot shift the narrow dimensions through which his character is rendered. While the heroes grapple with (the impossibility of) the ideal of an ethical cosmopolitanism and the seriousness of high modernism this brings, their predicaments are narrated according to the character typology of popular cinema.

The geographies of the center and of the peripheries presented in the three films cohere through the cosmopolitan subjectivity of the Danish male who traverses this global inequity. The stylistic codes that portray the movement between Denmark and other locales reinforce perceptually the importance of this movement for the male subject. In *Brothers,* the disjuncture between Denmark and Afghanistan is frequently highlighted in the way scenes move directly between the dark, enclosed space of Michael's cell as he becomes increasingly disconsolate and the light, sparsely furnished domestic spaces of his family's house, filled with children and activity. In some respects, this is a movement between the contrasting realities experienced by Michael in Afghanistan and Jannick in Denmark. By the time Jacob travels back to Copenhagen in the early scenes of *After the Wedding*, the viewer is already aware of his disdain for the Denmark he has left behind. One of the children at the orphanage asks Jacob before he leaves: "Are there only rich people where you are going? . . . If I were rich I'd be happy." Jacob replies: "I know, but people there are idiots." The child responds: "You always hate rich people, Mr. Jacob." India is shown as impoverished but with rich hues filling the frame, connoting vibrancy and immediacy. The children who are the focus of Jacob's life there thematically amplify this richness. The camera soon turns to the hotel room that has been reserved for Jacob when he arrives in Copenhagen. It is elegant but cold, and Jacob, once alone and looking uncomfortably out of place, tinkers with the flat-screen television and the electric blinds as if they are unknown to him.

The movement between worlds in *In a Better World* is more nuanced than in the trilogy's other two films. The color palettes that mark Africa and rural Denmark in summer are only subtly different. More than once, the shift from one locale to another is achieved by framing the landscape of the camp against the horizon with a slow dissolve into the hazy horizon of a field in the European country town at dusk. Yet, again, the movement between locales mirrors Anton's psyche and his geographical mobility; his experience unfolds as the story of the two comparable horizons. The transition between center and peripheries occurs differently in each film, almost mirroring how the men perceive the values of these places (for example, through light and dark), but in each case it is structured by the male sojourner's knowledge and psyche.

The greater portion of each sojourner's time is spent in small-town or suburban Denmark. When he returns from his work on the global stage, the protagonist struggles to reconcile his experiences abroad with the demands of the domestic sphere. Bier's preference for melodrama not only produces character typing, it also subverts the solemn resolve of the male characters. Seriousness is undercut by either uncontrolled emotion or the awkwardness and lack of certitude with which each protagonist navigates his personal relationships with daughters and lovers. All three seem unable to come to terms with the sites of Danish domesticity that should enable their patriarchal positions. Instead, they mumble and guess at how to proceed, as intimate conversations take place in well-furnished kitchens, bedrooms, and living rooms that accentuate the mundane. This is shown starkly in a scene in *After the Wedding* in which Jacob visits Helene at her home to demand information about Jørgen's plans. It is the first time they have spoken since they parted years before, and the conversation is stilted, moving from angry clumsiness to a fond exchange. Jacob accuses the wealthy Helene of "having no ideals" but soon allows her the intimacy of questioning him about his marital status. In another scene Jørgen breaks down and wails with startling intensity at the prospect of his impending death. Just as women in melodrama historically have been required to wrestle with their designated proper place in society given the social tensions staged across the domestic sphere, the men in Bier's trilogy are thrown into situations where they must engage with the tangled expectations of class, gender, and the everyday. Posing the female director alongside this melodramatic construction of masculine selfhood and its manifestation in the pursuit of ethical cosmopolitanism engenders the possibility of understanding this representation as a critique of such masculine endeavors.

The desire that drives the movement from the domestic to the worldly, and thus the ideal of good conduct in the humanitarian sector, gives a particular perspective to histories of colonialism and imperialism. The sojourner represents neither the colonizer nor the tourist but rather constitutes the new figure of the aid worker or peacekeeping soldier. He embodies the project of humanitarianism that, in Fuyuki Kurasawa's words, "has become one of the principal manifestations of the liberal democratic project in the post–Cold War world."[28] The project that facilitates the transnational flow of workers and soldiers from affluent nations also signals an expanding mode of liberal democratic humanism based in empathy and a discourse of human rights. Bier's trilogy takes a

Western worldview of its "othered" spaces: Afghanistan is equated with the chaos and violence of war, sub-Saharan Africa with civil war and ethnic cleansing, India with poverty and urban slums. As Kurasawa observes, images of suffering and war in the zones of the third world contribute to a "humanitarian scopic regime, a set of visual patterns, and a mode of representing distant suffering that structure Western perceptions of the global South and its inhabitants, as well as the range and kind of the Euro-American world's moral concern" (136). While Kurasawa is referring largely to a nonfiction visualization of the other, primarily in journalism, Bier's fictionalized images contribute to this "humanitarian scopic regime." Already informed by existing visual culture, the trilogy brings us three protagonists invested in humanitarian efforts in the developing world. This humanitarianism is especially aligned with the Northern European social democratic ethos.

The male sojourner and his experiences present a decisive way of placing these films in the contemporary world, the world of post–Cold War European liberal democracy. In one respect, the films take up the challenge of calling our attention to global inequity and sites of distant suffering. Such inequity shapes their point of view, and the viewer is invited to identify with their mission. Vision is crucial to this approach: each male sojourner's point of view is signified in scenes of transition between the distant sites in ways that mirror his visual perceptions. In addition to motion, the visual cues that indicate passage between the locations in Denmark and the zones of the periphery indicate where each sojourner's emotional and ethical compass is most powerfully directed. A specific and nuanced exploration of these sites necessarily remains beyond the scope of each film's plot. Rather, the question of how to act in the films' crisis-ridden environments comes to the fore—a question conjured by the challenges of an ideal ethical cosmopolitanism rendered as a masculine endeavor. This challenge burdens the male characters; not only must they undertake humanitarian missions abroad, they are also tasked with upholding and legitimizing patriarchal positions at home.

The films overburden their male protagonists with both the trials of domestic melodrama and the weight of Western ethical responsibility. The "humanitarian scopic regime" reinforces the subjective cosmopolitan position, albeit in ways that align the viewer with a singular, Western point of view. Individualized ethical identity—the Nordic characters are starkly individualized visually in the films' non-European settings—brings into focus and reflects questions that are pertinent to a national or regional Northern European psyche. While overtly political in theme, Bier's films center on the European imaginary and the role of both humanitarianism and the violence and/or suffering of the other in defining or transforming the (male) self.

Conclusion
Bier's films and her directorial image demonstrate symbolic and material mobility. Her films traverse the global cinema circuit and frequently cross genre categories. Furthermore, they negotiate a space between mass crossover appeal and cultural specificity. Her trilogy takes the viewer places, following traveling characters to locations that exceed the comforts of Danish affluence. Yet despite this global reach, the trilogy presents the global South in ways that highlight a Eurocentric worldview.

This essay has expanded on two different ways of perceiving the worlds of Bier, or, more specifically, the worlds her films produce. The notion of *film worlds* reconciles the two frames that have been the basis for my analysis. It includes the world signified by the narrative and formal structures of the film and the world that expands around the film, produced and organized by constellations of films, markets, categories of criticism, and the predilections of taste and cultural capital. Both worlds position the figure of the director discursively. In Bier's trilogy, these worlds coincide around the trope of the European male sojourner, an allegorical figure that facilitates the address to the global or transnational cinema audience. Yet what is at stake in foregrounding this figure?

It may be that the moral questioning with regard to the contemporary currency of humanitarian cosmopolitanism in Bier's films functions superficially to affirm the sensibilities of the arthouse audience consuming foreign-language cinema. After all, the plight of the other, most clearly rendered in *In a Better World* and *After the Wedding*, is already known to the audience and serves only to complement the journey of the protagonist while the other's subjectivity or the forces at play in global hegemonies are not registered within the films. Yet perhaps to read the figure of the female director alongside these allegories of good conduct is also to perceive their value as reflexive meditations on the problem of Western masculine sociality.

Reading Bier's cinema as popular melodrama offers an opportunity to understand not only how it has been feminized as "lite" art film but also how it imitates and critiques the hero of modernist cinema. The manner in which the sojourner negotiates the quotidian is highlighted in the melodramatic codes of the films and subverts his high modernist status.

It is instructive to return to the historical "problem of the world" identified by McHugh, one that recognizes "women's compromised relation to legacy."[29] The negative legacy of women is their lack of authority over space and lack of the material opportunities that authority engenders. Woolf's reference to the "whole world" signals a platform for addressing this legacy of lack, a forum that bypasses other spatialities like the nation or the private sphere. Bier's trilogy critiques this legacy, appropriating transnational mobility at the level of narrative and audience address and employing these as tools to interrogate the outward-looking cosmopolitanism of late modernity.

The male characters stand in this respect not as ideals but rather as signs of the dominance of the Western imaginary. Cosmopolitan subjectivity is central to this problematic. As I have noted, cosmopolitanism encompasses an ethical aspiration for political rights that are not confined within territorial borders. It also describes psychical and physical mobility and the particular self-knowledge they afford. In *Brothers*, *In a Better World*, and *After the Wedding*, the distinct visual qualities that convey movement between cultures and emphasize mobility do not extend to offering a fully realized ethical engagement. Rather than reiterating the mastery of vision as the purview of the Western masculine subject alone, however, Bier's popular cinema might be perceived as one that poses its protagonists' experiences at home and in the world for a mass audience. The fallibility and impotence of Bier's male sojourner focus attention on the limitations of his vision and the Eurocentric imagination. Given that the auteur has been by default historically constructed as masculine, it may be that exposing this fantasy of vision and mastery presents a critique not only of the Eurocentric imagination and its manifestation in art cinema but also of the gendered assumptions that frame the director's signature.

Notes

1. See, for example, Belinda Smaill, "Sofia Coppola: Reading the Director," *Feminist Media Studies* 13, no. 1 (2013): 148–62; Deb Verhoeven, *Jane Campion* (London: Routledge, 2009); Lingzhen Wang, ed., *Chinese Women's Cinema: Transnational Contexts* (New York: Columbia University Press, 2011); Patricia White, "Global Flows of Women's Cinema: Nadine Labaki and Female Authorship," in *Media Authorship*, ed. Cynthia Chris and David A. Gerstner (London: Routledge, 2013), 212–28; and Patricia White, *Women's Cinema/World Cinema: Projecting Twenty-First-Century Feminisms* (Durham, NC: Duke University Press, forthcoming).

2. Virginia Woolf, quoted in Kathleen McHugh, "The World and the Soup: Historicizing Media Feminisms in Transnational Contexts," *Camera Obscura*, no. 72 (2009): 111.

3. McHugh, "World and the Soup," 112, 113.

4. Thomas Elsaesser, *European Cinema: Face to Face with Hollywood* (Amsterdam: Amsterdam University Press, 2005), 498.

5. The most conspicuous example is Kathryn Bigelow. While her work has been examined in relation to questions of gender, her public statements shy away from feminism.

6. It is significant that in many national industries, women are overrepresented in the television industry when compared with cinema. In reference to the US situation, Christina Lane writes that although women frequently find this sphere to be a springboard for feature film production, many return to

television after directing features when they can no longer secure work in Hollywood. For those aspiring to a career directing feature films, returning to television may be a second choice that allows them to continue working in the industry. Since Lane's account of the industry was published, however, the production of quality television has intensified. The quality television brand has been successful in attracting film directors, including notable women, who are interested in working in this sphere. See Christina Lane, *Feminist Hollywood: From "Born in Flames" to "Point Break"* (Detroit: Wayne State University Press, 2000), 229.

7. For a fuller discussion of the emergence of a transnational communicative Nordic space, see Mette Hjort, *Small Nation, Global Cinema: The New Danish Cinema* (Minneapolis: University of Minnesota Press, 2005).

8. Terry Gross, "Filmmaker Susanne Bier, Seeking 'A Better World,'" NPR, 10 March 2011, m.npr.org/news/Arts+%26+Life/134391928.

9. Mette Hjort, "Susanne Bier," in *The Danish Directors: Dialogues on a Contemporary National Cinema*, ed. Mette Hjort and Ib Bondebjerg (Bristol, UK: Intellect, 2001), 242.

10. Susanne Bier, "Susanne Bier Interviewed by Jason Wood," in *Projections 13: Women Filmmakers on Filmmaking*, ed. Isabella Weibrecht and John Boorman (London: Faber and Faber, 2004), 98.

11. Hjort, "Susanne Bier," 245–46.

12. Louise Kidde Sauntved, "Sudden Impact: The Catastrophic Tales and Booming Career of Susanne Bier," *Film Comment* 47, no. 2 (2011): 25.

13. Richard Dyer and Ginette Vincendeau, introduction to *Popular European Cinema*, ed. Richard Dyer and Ginette Vincendeau (London: Routledge, 1992), 2.

14. Victor Perkins, "The Atlantic Divide," in Dyer and Vincendeau, *Popular European Cinema*, 196.

15. Hjort, "Susanne Bier," 246.

16. Dimitris Eleftheriotis, *Popular Cinemas of Europe: Studies of Texts, Contexts, and Frameworks* (New York: Continuum, 2001), 68.

17. Manohla Dargis, "Shifty Wedding Crashers: Secrets from the Past," *New York Times*, 30 March 2007.

18. David Fear, "*In a Better World*," *Time Out New York*, 28 March 2011.

19. Meryl Shriver-Rice, "Adapting National Identity: Ethical Borders Made Suspect in the Hollywood Version of Susanne Bier's *Brothers*," *Film International* 9, no. 2 (2011): 14.

20. Margaret Pomeranz, "Review of *After the Wedding*," At the Movies, abc.net.au/atthemovies/txt/s1983684.htm (accessed July 2013).

21. Kidde Sauntved, "Sudden Impact," 24–27.

22. Robert Sklar, "*In a Better World*," *Cineaste* 36, no. 3 (2011): 48; Fear, "*In a Better World*."

23. David Edelstein, "The Dullness of Being Earnest," *New York Magazine*, 27 March 2011.

24. As Patricia White notes, though, films with female leads that are offered comparable marketing budgets "will succeed at the same rate as those headlined by men." Patricia White, "Watching Women's Films," *Camera Obscura*, no. 72 (2009): 154.

25. Mette Hjort, *Lone Scherfig's "Italian for Beginners"* (Seattle: University of Washington Press, 2010), 23.

26. Michel Foucault, *Ethics: Subjectivity and Truth*, ed. Paul Rabinow, trans. Robert Hurley, in *Essential Works of Foucault, 1954–1984*, vol. 1 (London: Penguin, 1997), 88.

27. Nikos Papastergiadis, *Cosmopolitanism and Culture* (Cambridge: Polity, 2012), 136.

28. Fuyuki Kurasawa, "Humanitarianism and the Representation of Alterity: The Aporias and Prospects of Cosmopolitan Visuality," in *Democracy in Crisis: Violence, Alterity, Community*, ed. Stella Gaon (Manchester: Manchester University Press, 2009), 135.

29. McHugh, "World and the Soup," 113.

Belinda Smaill is a senior lecturer in film and television studies at Monash University. She is the author of *The Documentary: Politics, Emotion, Culture* (Palgrave Macmillan, 2010) and coauthor, with Audrey Yue and Olivia Khoo, of *Transnational Australian Cinema: Ethics in the Asian Diasporas* (Lexington, 2013). Her essays have appeared in a range of journals, including *Quarterly Review of Film and Video, Camera Obscura, Feminist Media Studies,* and *Continuum.*

Figure 3. *Brothers* (*Brødre*, dir. Susanne Bier, Denmark, 2004)

Figure 1. Theatrical poster for *Dirty Bitch* (*Tu Nu* [兔女], dir. Sun Koh, Singapore, 2009)

The Minor Transnationalism of Queer Asian Cinema: Female Authorship and the Short Film Format

Olivia Khoo

Critical approaches to Asian women directors are shaped within the evolving disciplinary formation of Asian cinema, which so far has privileged auteurism as the dominant framework in defining the cinema against its Euro-American counterparts. Although there have been, and continue to be, important works recuperating lost or marginalized female auteurs throughout the history of Asian cinema, much of this work has been conducted in the context of national film histories, making it difficult to draw meaningful connections outside such a framework. Investment in the figure of the male auteur—Zhang Yimou, Hou Hsiao-Hsien, Wong Kar-wai, Park Chan-wook, and Apichatpong Weerasethakul, for example—and his success in the international arena privileges modernist, arthouse cinema. As Lingzhen Wang argues, the films that are valued on the international circuit "endorse depoliticization, aesthetic transcendence, and an indifferent cosmopolitan style, and dismiss the significance of gender and alternative histories."[1]

Queer cinema constitutes a more politicized international dimension of contemporary Asian cinema, and some of the most vibrant and interesting work currently produced by women in Asia can be located within queer cinema. Yet, again, most of the high-profile directors associated with queer Asian cinema are men (such as Stanley Kwan, Tsai Ming-liang, and Cui Zi'en), in part because they have made feature films. The contributions to queer Asian cinema of women filmmakers—many having had long careers in television and documentary and short film production—have not been as visible as those of their male counterparts unless or until they break onto the scene with a feature film.

Thus the female director within queer Asian cinema is marked by an in-betweenness that in many cases renders her invisible. She is caught between national cinema formations and the institutional flows of world cinema (the desire to attract a local audience while also aspiring to the film festival circuit) and between commercial and independent imperatives (the requirement to make a career out of filmmaking despite carrying the limiting labels of Asian, woman, and/or queer). These tensions are registered in the reception of different formats of filmmaking, with feature film production being regarded as a primary marker of critical and/or commercial success. Far from devaluing non–feature film production, this essay seeks to examine the importance of the short film format for an understanding of women's contributions to Asian cinema generally and queer Asian cinema in particular. I pay attention to how the unique qualities of the short film format allow Asian women filmmakers to actively engage with each other's work within and across the region and how this transnational connection is redefining how we understand the figure of the individual auteur of women's filmmaking.

In this essay I examine the particular industrial and institutional contexts for a commissioned short film from Singapore, Sun Koh's *Dirty Bitch* (*Tu Nu* [兔女], 2009), tracing the production and circulation of this film to explore how female authorship might be productively reconceptualized by drawing upon the in-betweenness that has so far rendered it invisible. Focusing on the context of Singaporean cinema, a minor or small national cinema, I explore how this particular local, authorial example highlights the need to make transnational connections from production to reception, situating this discussion within women's film culture and Asian queer culture as a form of minor transnationalism.

The Short Film Form and Singapore's Minor Cinema

The contemporary film industry in Singapore experienced a revival in the 1990s following a period of dormancy between 1973 and 1991, during which not a single recorded feature film was made on the island. After independence from Malaysia, the country was consumed by the process of rapid industrialization, turning back to supporting local film culture only in the 1990s. Some forty-five feature films were made in the period between 1991 and 2004. Singapore's film revival was the product of a combination of public and private initiatives: state-sponsored scholarships for Singaporeans to study film abroad, funding for training at local polytechnics, and the establishment in 1998 of the Singapore Film Commission and the production company Raintree Pictures. Since the revival, Singaporean cinema has been successful in the realm of short filmmaking.

Singapore's short film production has grown since 2000 as a result of government financial support through the Singapore Film Commission and because short films are allowed to feature in a competitive category at the Singapore International Film Festival. This in turn has paved the way for the success of Singaporean shorts at other major international festivals, including Cannes and Rotterdam. Film scholars Jan Uhde and Yvonne Ng Uhde note that "short films have significantly contributed to the development of Singapore cinema as a whole."[2] Whereas in some national film industries it is difficult to obtain funding for short films because of low prospects for a return, in Singapore short films receive funding because they are seen as a stepping-stone to success in the feature film industry and thus as a way of nurturing local talent to achieve success internationally.[3]

A short film is generally classified in terms of its length, usually under sixty minutes in running time. The temporal aspect of characterizing the short film, however, does not account for the range of techniques, styles, and themes that the format can create, nor for the variety of short films and the diverse professional and institutional functions for which they are made: from calling-card shorts and commissioned shorts to independent, avant-garde experiments for alternative exhibition circuits.

Nick Deocampo outlines the short film's characteristics as "*brevity, unity* (or singularity of theme, character, or technique), *variety of form*, and a *large degree of creative freedom*."[4] Uhde and Uhde add: "As the short is not a format used for general commercial release, it is less subject to censorship control and therefore allows for greater artistic freedom and experimentation, an advantage especially important in tightly controlled Singapore."[5] Short films enable filmmakers to debate issues in Singaporean society that might otherwise remain unremarked. Young Singapore-born filmmaker Sun Koh (born 1977), whose short film *Dirty Bitch* forms the focus of this essay, has used the short format on several occasions to challenge the constraints of public discourse in Singapore. Koh's *The Secret Heaven* (2002), which recounts the fantasies of a young girl wanting to escape her piano lessons, comments on the pressure put on Singaporean children by their parents to perform well. Another short made by Koh, *Bedroom Dancing* (2006), explores issues of isolation, voyeurism, and lack of privacy in Singapore's public Housing Development Board flats, and was inspired by a criminal case in which a man was arrested and fined S$6,500 for masturbating in his own apartment.

Queer Singaporean filmmakers have especially embraced the short film form. The higher-profile filmmakers of this cinema—including Loo Zi-han, Royston Tan, and Boo Junfeng—are men.[6] Singapore has only produced one full-length gay feature film to date, Loo Zi-han's *Solos* (2007). The short film form has afforded queer filmmakers a greater degree of artistic freedom in negotiating issues of censorship relating to sexuality, and several women filmmakers, including Eva Tang (*Londres-London* [UK, 2006]) and Kirsten Han (Spudnik Productions), have had success with their queer-themed short films. The Substation, an arts center founded in Singapore in 1990, has provided an important space for screening and nurturing the short film scene, in particular through its Short Circuit program and annual Singapore Short Film Awards. The inaugural Short Circuit film festival in October 2006 featured twelve short films that either were produced by lesbian, gay, bisexual, and transgender (LGBT) individuals or featured an LGBT theme.[7] This is a notable event in the context of the young and relatively small—that is, minor—queer film scene in Singapore.

Singapore is not the only Southeast Asian nation to become known for its short films. An article by producer Juan Foo titled "Mini Cinema" argues that "a nation's cinema starts with shorts," emphasizing the importance of this form to many of the smaller film industries in Southeast Asia.[8] Writing on the contemporary short film movement in the Philippines, Deocampo argues that it constitutes a new Philippine cinema, marking a period distinct from the 1970s commercial and independent cinema in the country. Deocampo notes that the format of the short film has been taken up fervently by youth in the Philippines since the 1980s; the short, however, still remains critically and popularly marginalized in relation to the nation's commercial cinema. Deocampo characterizes the short film in the Philippines as a "submerged cinema" that has always existed as the "other" to commercial cinema, with "its own history, aesthetics, ideology, and practicing filmmakers."[9] He argues that "a counter-culture results from this tenacity to survive despite prevailing hindrances like rising costs, absence of a 'professional system' to sustain film production and distribution, competition from commercial films and video, and an audience that has yet to be tapped" (vii). While Singapore's short filmmaking culture is not the avant-garde oppositional culture Deocampo finds in the Philippines, the short film's tenacity for commercial survival in Singapore underscores this form as an integral mode of filmmaking in light of current economic realities of film production, distribution, and exhibition. For a minor film industry like Singapore, short films become an important mode of entry into major cinema circuits, including those of elite international film festivals.

Drawing from Gilles Deleuze and Félix Guattari's use of the term *minor literature* in their study *Kafka: Toward a Minor Literature*, Tom Gunning has noted the appearance of a new form of avant-garde cinema during the late 1980s that he calls "minor cinema."[10] Gunning defines minor films as those that "recognize their marginal identity and consciously maintain a position outside the major cinematic languages." Minor films are "creatively parasitic" and often oppositional, in the sense of not holding aspirations of a commercial breakthrough.[11] The relationship between the commercial and the creative is more fully emphasized in the context of Singapore's emergent film industry, where generous government funding does demand a return, however implicitly, making it a requirement for filmmakers to engage the minor in cinema in ever more creative ways.

Valuable rearticulations of the concept of minor cinema have accounted for the transnational circuits of women's cinema and queer cinema, highlighting the gendered dimensions of the term *minor* and reclaiming the pejorative connotations associated with its gendering. These rearticulations include Alison Butler's consideration of contemporary women's cinema as a form of minor cinema and Patricia White's study of short-form commissioned works in her essay "Lesbian Minor Cinema."[12] Like Gunning, both Butler and White draw from Deleuze and Guattari's notion of *minor literature*. Butler observes that women's cinema "now seems 'minor' rather than oppositional" and develops a connection between Deleuze and Guattari's notion of *collective enunciation* and her characterization of women's cinema as a minor cinema. Because a minor literature or cinema emerges from a deterritorialized group, it conjures up collective implications "even in the absence of an active community."[13] Beyond a reconceptualization of authorship that such an approach offers, Butler cautions on the continued need to engage "the major"—issues of funding, production, and distribution.

Paying particular attention to these questions of the global movement of capital and the reception of queer women's cinema, White considers how lesbian filmmakers deploy the notion of *the minor* in imaginative and generative ways. While White does not posit a direct equivalence between Deleuze and Guattari's notion of *the minor* and the concept of *queer*, she finds productive resonances between the two, understanding minor cinema "most straightforwardly as making use of limited resources in a politicized way."[14] By embracing the minor (for example, in the use of video rather than film or by making short-format works instead of features), lesbian filmmakers demonstrate their resourcefulness in negotiating major languages, genres, and national cinemas from which their work might otherwise be excluded. White notes that short-format work in particular "circumvents the commodity circulation and narrative boundedness of the feature film, crossing into other communities and contexts such as . . . festival networks" (413).

The important role that film festivals play in the exhibition of queer short films is especially pertinent to queer Asian cinema, which remains, as Helen Hok-Sze Leung notes, predominantly a festival category, unlike New Queer Cinema in the United States, which was rapidly mainstreamed.[15] Queer Asian cinema produced by women filmmakers can be located between specialist queer film festivals and women's film festivals, and occasionally as part of elite art festivals. This particular distribution and exhibition framework presents a need to consider not only the transnational production of queer Asian cinema produced by women but also its reception.

Butler notes that while comparative, cross-cultural analyses in film studies are still relatively new, in the field of women's studies transnational critical practice is more influential and widely accepted.[16] Yet while transnational approaches in film studies may be nascent, their use has nowhere been more fervent than in the context of Asian cinemas. As Will Higbee and Song Hwee Lim suggest, transnationalism is fast becoming a "default concept" when discussing (East) Asian cinemas.[17] Higbee and Lim argue for a "critical transnationalism" in film studies that remains attuned to both the loose usage and the overvaluation of the term *trans-*

nationalism (7). Wang, meanwhile, reengages long-standing debates of transnational feminism and links them to film scholarship in the introduction to her collection *Chinese Women's Cinema: Transnational Contexts*. Wang writes: "Today, feminist film studies must step outside the restrictive framework of the nation-state and critically resituate gender and cinema in a transnational feminist configuration that enables the examination of relationships of power and knowledge among and within cultures and nation-states."[18] Transnational film feminism, in its most critical form, does not privilege Western film feminisms or consider Asian film feminisms as temporally coming after Western film debates. The applicability of Western film feminisms to the Asian context is questionable, as access to Western feminist theories, including feminist film theories, has been uneven in Asia and in some places almost nonexistent.[19] Rather, transnational feminism's relevance to Asian cinema is that it emphasizes political links—"political rather than biological or cultural bases for alliance."[20] What emerges out of these connections is a rich network of women filmmakers and filmmaking practices spanning short films, documentaries, animation, and video work as opposed to a dominant narrative of nation-states or of prominent auteurs lauded at major international film festivals. By exploring these connections between women filmmakers and their work in Singapore and beyond, it is possible to rethink the notion of female authorship in relation to Asian cinema as something less individualized and more politicized. The short works of female directors in Singapore—including Koh, Eva Tang, Jasmine Ng Kin-Kia, and Kaz Cai —need to be regarded as part of a wider, coterminous development of independent filmmaking by women in the Asian region.[21] Considered in this light, women's filmmaking within Asian cinema, and in particular queer Asian cinema, can most accurately be described as a form of minor transnationalism.

Françoise Lionnet and Shu-mei Shih describe minor transnationalism as a specific intervention into dominant conceptions of transnationalism "from above." They write: "Major discussions of transnationalism and globalization assume that ethnic particularity and minoritized perspectives are contained within and easily assimilated into the dominant forms of transnationalism. . . . What is lacking in the binary model of above-and-below, the utopic and the dystopic, and the global and the local is an awareness and recognition of the creative interventions that networks of minoritized cultures produce within and across national boundaries." Not only does minor transnationalism consist of minority cultural articulations with a majority culture, it also encompasses minor-to-minor articulations within and across national borders.[22] Examining short films by women in Asia also foregrounds the minor transnationalism of queer Asian circuits, because queer Asian cinema produced by women filmmakers is the category most routinely excluded from the feature film and auteurist terrain of major international film festivals. Through an analysis of *Dirty Bitch*, I explore not only how Singapore's minor cinema engages with the major circulations of elite international film festivals but also how the minor-to-minor transnational connections between women filmmakers and queer film cultures in Asia enable a reimagining of traditional forms of film authorship.

Dirty Bitch

After studying mass communication at Ngee Ann Polytechnic and working for several years as a director of television documentaries, dramas, infotainment, and commercials in Singapore, Koh made the transition from commercial to independent work. Her first short film, *Secret Heaven*, performed well internationally and was the first Singaporean film to win a major award (the Silver Hugo) at the Chicago International Film Festival. Koh also won Best Director at the Fifteenth Singapore International Film Festival. Koh's later short *Dirty Bitch* was commissioned by the Rotterdam International Film Festival as part of "Meet the Maestro: Claire Denis" in 2009, screening alongside the premiere of Denis's *35 Rhums* (*35 Shots of Rum* [France/Germany, 2008]). *Dirty Bitch* was the only short to be so commissioned.[23]

As Koh notes in the opening intertitles, *Dirty Bitch* was inspired by a "violently censored" VHS copy of Denis's *Nénette et Boni* (France, 1996) that she found at Singapore's public performing arts library at the Esplanade. The film is both an homage to and a whimsical reinterpretation of Denis's gritty and poetic feature film. *Dirty Bitch* has achieved a small measure of success locally and internationally through the film festival circuit, with critics praising its brazen visuals and unexpectedly comedic representation of youthful sexual desire and violence. Film critic Chris Fujiwara comments, "At fourteen minutes, the film has more ideas than most features."[24]

Nénette et Boni, the tale of a fraught yet ultimately tender relationship between a brother and sister, is transplanted in *Dirty Bitch* from a rundown house in Marseille to a public housing flat in Singapore. Sexual imagery involving baguettes and coffee percolators in the Denis original finds substitutes in a bowl of instant noodles, and brother-sister disagreements become physicalized in a slow-motion sumo wrestling match. A young police constable, Chen Ming Jun (Kevin Tan), narrates, in Mandarin-language voice-over, his desire for a female colleague. He berates his sister, Chen Ming Zhen (Serene Chen), for returning to the family home pregnant. Zhen is determined to keep the "dirty secret" of her unwanted pregnancy from everyone and violently silences anyone who might expose her. In fantastical interludes, she pokes out her brother's eyes and cuts out the tongue of her gynecologist.

All of this is humorously portrayed in vibrant color and imagery and with exaggerated performances. Interspersed in the film is a musical segment featuring a dominatrix gynecologist played by Loretta Chen, who lip-synchs an upbeat French rap song (written and performed by Anne-Laure Sibon, finalist on *Star Academy*). Accompanying the song is a further animated sequence featuring the Merlion—a Singapore landmark with the head of a lion and the body of a fish—which spits out Kewpie dolls into the Singapore River as more dolls dance around other tourist landmarks. The gynecologist tells Zhen that it is too late for her to have an abortion and proceeds to whip the pregnant girl's bottom. Finally, one of the Kewpie dolls is flattened by a shoe and the animated musical segment ends as blood splatters and slowly drips away. In the final scene of the film, Zhen, now heavily pregnant, is being interviewed for entry into law school. Her interviewers (played by Fanny Kee, Ken Sun, and Kenneth Paul Tan) begin

Figures 2–3. Kewpie dolls representing the protagonist's unwanted pregnancy. *Dirty Bitch*

asking her questions in English. As Zhen stumbles on her answers, music fades in and the interviewers rise from their seats and begin laughing, drinking beer, and dancing in blood-splattered white bunny slippers as the film concludes.

Dirty Bitch has not generally been read or positioned as a queer text—it has not, for example, screened at any queer film festivals—but I read the film's queer potential not only in its camp appeal but also in terms of how it provokes a rethinking of female authorship within a minor transnational network of women's short filmmaking and queer Asian cinema. *Dirty Bitch* resonates aesthetically and thematically with the early short films of one of Singapore's best-known independent documentary filmmakers, Tan Pin Pin, arguably more than it represents an homage to the stylistic qualities of Denis's original film. While Tan Pin Pin's short films and documentaries also do not explicitly reference queer subjectivity, two of her short fiction films can be read as queer through their deployment of a camp aesthetic and use of Barbie doll figurines in the tradition of Todd Haynes's *Superstar: The Karen Carpenter Story* (US, 1987). Tan Pin Pin's *Lurve Me Now* (1999), a three-minute short that portrays the sexual fantasies of a Barbie doll, was banned by the Singaporean government for its suggestive sexual content. *Microwave* (2000), a two-and-a-half-minute short film with the simple yet effective premise of a Barbie doll placed in a rotating microwave oven, is an even more condensed example of the unusual blend of comedy, camp, and suppressed sexualized violence to which *Dirty Bitch* pays tribute. Tan Pin Pin's films also do not circulate on queer film festival circuits; the queerness of

Lurve Me Now and *Microwave* is primarily a matter of interpretation, although the films themselves are open and experimental and invite multiple perspectives and interaction with audiences.

In reading *Dirty Bitch* and Tan Pin Pin's early short films as queer texts, I draw on Helen Hok-Sze Leung's notion of *queerscapes*. Writing in the context of Hong Kong cinema and the recent proliferation of works featuring new expressions of sexuality and sexual identity, Leung introduces the term *queerscape* to avoid passing judgment on which representations should be regarded as legitimately queer, for example by essentializing a queer perspective or what might be considered authentic queer subjectivity. Leung writes: "Queerscapes refer to the contingent and tangential uses of public space by sexual minorities and to public acts and expressions of desire, eroticism, and sexuality that momentarily disrupt what heterocentric ideology assumes to be an immutable, coherent relation between biological sex, gender, and sexual desire." Queerscapes refer "not only to gay and lesbian spaces, but also to all spaces that challenge heteronormativity."[25] Leung's idea of queerscapes introduces a more fluid definition of *queer* as a critical concept in relation to film texts since it does not rely on the identity of the filmmaker or even of the film's subjects. Rather, "queer" becomes "an analytical framework to look for what denaturalizes, disrupts, or resignifies the relation conventionally drawn between gendered embodiments, erotic desire, and sexual identities."[26] Within such a framework, it also becomes possible, and indeed useful, to align a queer spectatorial position and methodology with the minor transnationalism of women's filmmaking in Singapore and in the region beyond. It is this minor cinema in Asia of short films by women that in turn highlights and articulates with the minor transnational circuits of Singapore's cinematic queerscapes.

Instead of reproducing the kind of realist arthouse film privileged by the elite international film festival circuit—including Rotterdam, for which it was commissioned—as Denis's film arguably does, Koh has instead produced a short comedy "about facing your inner bunny" (as the film's tagline states). Boni's pet rabbit in the Denis original has become, in Koh's version, a pair of blood-splattered fluffy white bunny slippers worn by the violent female protagonist, the "dirty bitch" of the film's title.

In contrast to the film's provocative English title, its Chinese title, *Tu Nu*, translates literally as "rabbit girl." While the figure of the rabbit

Figure 4. *Dirty Bitch* title card

can be seen as a reference to the animal's perceived reproductive promiscuity ("breeding like rabbits"), it has another connotation: *rabbit (tuzi)* was a slang term for homosexuals used in late imperial China, and the term continues to connote homoeroticism in particular Fujian-speaking Chinese communities, where gay men are still sometimes referred to as "rabbits."[27] Historically, this terminology can be traced to a folktale recounted in the *Zi Bu Yu*, a book written by Qing dynasty scholar and poet Yuan Mei, about a man named Hu Tianbao, who became known as the Rabbit God. Hu Tianbao, as the story goes, fell in love with an imperial inspector of Fujian Province. He was caught spying on the inspector; when he confessed his infatuation, he was sentenced to death. The judges of the underworld, learning that his crime was one of love, appointed him patron god of homosexuals and safeguard of homosexual affections.[28] He was posthumously deified as Tu Er Shen, the Rabbit God, and a temple was dedicated to his worship in Yonghe, Taiwan.[29] Because this historical reference is not commonly known outside Fujian-speaking communities or Chinese homosexual communities, it highlights the minor transnational circuits of queer Asian cultures in which the film circulates. *Dirty Bitch* connects the folktale's symbolism of the rabbit in the film's Chinese title with the reclamation of a word considered derogatory to women in its English title. Although the folktale does not explicitly reference female homosexuality, and while the director may not have intended the rabbit figure to be a queer reference, I argue that the connotation of homosexuality carries over through the film's pervasive deployment of the symbol, which can be read as queer.

In *Nénette et Boni*, the film's point of view is aligned with the brother, Boni (Grégoire Colin). Although the brother's heterosexual fantasy also frames the opening of *Dirty Bitch*, the film itself, as I argue, is pervasively queer.[30] From the imagery of the camp dominatrix to the queer symbolism of the rabbit, Koh's film can be read as a queer text that, as Teresa de Lauretis describes, "not only works against narrativity, the generic pressure of all narrative toward closure and the fulfilment of meaning, but also pointedly disrupts the referentiality of language and the referentiality of images."[31] The loose narrative thread of *Dirty Bitch* is overlaid with suggestive imagery and potent symbolism removed from their usual referents. Kewpie dolls make an appearance in the camp, kitsch musical sequence but are transformed from a symbol of European domesticity to one representing Asian cute culture.[32] As a symbol of Zhen's unwanted baby, the Kewpie doll also represents Zhen's tainted future: she says to her gynecologist, "Cut it out! I won't have it come out and disgrace me!"

As the central motif of the film, Zhen's distaste toward her pregnancy invokes Lee Edelman's critique of the way in which the child is figured as the imaginary that secures the future, as "the emblem of futurity's unquestioned value."[33] José Esteban Muñoz, arguing conversely about the possibility of queerness as a utopic future, posits that queerness is primarily the realm of futurity and hope. Muñoz insists "on the essential need for an understanding of queerness as collectivity," echoing Butler's comments on women's (minor) cinema as a form of collective enunciation.[34] *Dirty Bitch* cleverly invites a play with these ideas: its heroine is a seemingly oppositional, isolated, and violent individual, but the film ultimately offers a celebration of the (queer) bonds between people. The fact that the film is inspired by Denis's film but is also a "love letter" to Singapore's censors creates a multilayered sense of the remake—of a work that is reproductive but also future oriented and open ended.[35]

Dirty Bitch engages in at least two kinds of transnationalism. One kind, more explicit and comprehensible, is its status as a remake and commissioned homage to a major French filmmaker and indeed icon of women's cinema, Denis. The other pertains to the film's circulation as part of a less visible, still not yet fully conceptualized minor transnational circuit of women's filmmaking in Asia, particularly as it articulates with the minor transnational circuit of queer Asian cinema. To view *Dirty Bitch* as merely an homage to the Denis original is to risk celebrating only the major transnational exchanges between West and East (France/the Netherlands and Singapore) and the institutional and funding structures that facilitate these dominant flows through elite film festivals such as Rotterdam, at the expense of recognizing the minor transnational networks of women's filmmaking and queer Asian cinema within which the film also circulates and that arguably offer a more productive critical frame. In addition to its debut at Rotterdam, *Dirty Bitch* also screened at the 2010 Women Make Waves Film Festival in Taiwan and at film festivals around Asia, including the Eleventh Cinemanila International Film Festival, Philippines; the Third Balinale International Film Festival, Indonesia; the Tenth Jeonju International Film Festival, South Korea; and the Fifth InDPanda International Short Film Festival, Hong Kong.

Implicit in a reading of the film as an example of minor transnationalism is a politics of affirmation that invites new collaborations to emerge out of what has come before. *Dirty Bitch* opens up precisely such critical explorations, using the future possibility of the child—figured through the protagonist's pregnancy—to engage women filmmakers' participation in (queer) Asian cinema as a form of potentiality. Rather than simply repeating or remaking Denis's film, Koh's film builds on it with references from Singapore cinema—especially Singaporean women's filmmaking, including the works of Tan Pin Pin—queer Asian cinema, and international art cinema, and in turn provides an invitation for others to respond to her film.

Koh's ethic of collaboration is also evident in her other filmmaking projects, including *Lucky 7*, the exquisite corpse feature for which she acted as executive producer in 2008. *Lucky 7* is directed by seven Singaporean filmmakers—Boo Junfeng, Chew Tze Chuan, Ho Tzu Nyen, Koh, K. Rajagopal, Tania Sng, and Brian Gothong Tan—four of whom are queer.[36] The film consists of seven segments, each one ten to twelve minutes in length. Each filmmaker was only permitted to watch the final minute of the segment preceding his or hers before making his or her own, building on what came before. The only element that does not change throughout the segments is the lead actor, Sunny Pang. Koh says of the film: "I wanted it to be a showcase of the filmmakers working in Singapore back then. Most important of all, it had to reflect the[ir] diversity. So the directors were chosen to be very different from each other. The directors also had to crew on each other's shoot, as a way of fostering active collaboration."[37] Koh regards collaboration as a circumstantial response to local conditions in the film industry: "We Singaporean directors are too isolated, working on our own instead of with each other. In contrast with Malaysia's independent filmmakers, who serve on each other's sets and collaborate to a greater degree. The film is experimental, but this allows greater collaboration between the independent filmmakers, allowing them to share ideas as well as technical skills, to complete a feature-length film."[38]

Although this example occurs within an ostensibly national film culture, the assumption of a national film culture belies the existence of a minor transnationalism at work not only within but also across national contexts. Koh is a strongly transnational filmmaker in the production, circulation, and exhibition of her films. She has been highly awarded at festivals internationally and is an alumna of the Berlinale Talent Campus (2003), Busan International Film Festival's Asian Film Academy (2007), and the Taipei Golden Horse Film Academy (2009). Koh is not unique among Singaporean directors in her international outlook. As a small nation in geopolitical terms, Singapore necessarily looks outward, and its international orientation can be seen in the many efforts and campaigns of the government's Media Development Authority to attract international collaborators—for example, by signing bilateral film coproduction agreements and sending local talent to be trained abroad before returning to work in the domestic industry. By invoking the collaborative nature of Malaysia's independent film scene, Koh also immediately raises comparisons between Singapore's independent filmmakers and their cross-straits counterparts.

Well beyond the national context, Koh has reprised the exquisite corpse format in a more recent filmic collaboration with six women directors in Sweden, where she was based from 2011 to

2013. The film, titled *Sweden 7/Sverige 7*, is a collaboration between Stina Bergman, Maja Borg, Elisabet Gustafsson, Koh, Tove Krabo, Jenifer Malmqvist, and Jessica Nettelbladt. The first segment of the film was crowd funded with the hope that the segment could then be used to obtain more funding from governmental and commercial sources.[39] From the success of her omnibus project in Singapore, Koh has been able to facilitate a minor-to-minor cinematic network between small-nation film industries and create an opportunity to engage Swedish funding sources. What Koh's filmmaking initiatives reveal is a creative embrace of in-betweenness as an attempt to create greater commercial opportunities from an otherwise independent film project and to go beyond the national context to explore transnational connections among women filmmakers.[40] By using the short film form in this way, Koh challenges the traditional meaning of female authorship, drawing on a minor transnational cinema network across Singapore and beyond.

Other women filmmakers in Singapore who employ similar strategies of collaboration in order to develop their creative projects out of a minor cinema include Kaz Cai, one of three female directors from Asia (along with Wang Jing from China and Anocha Suwichakornpong from Thailand) involved in the transnational omnibus film *Breakfast, Lunch, Dinner* (2010), and Eva Tang, director of the award-winning lesbian short *Londres-London*, who has reprised her collaboration with well-known local filmmakers Royston Tan and Victric Thng to make *Old Romances* (2013), a sequel to the three filmmakers' earlier *Old Places* (2010). Like Koh, Tang was born in Singapore but has lived and studied abroad in Hong Kong, London, and China, leaving a career in journalism to accept a scholarship from the Singapore Film Commission to study film in the UK. Her short film *While You Sleep* (2002) was shot in the UK and funded by both the British Council and the Singapore Film Commission, and features dialogue entirely in Japanese. Tang's career has also been shaped by success at major film forums. She was the first Singaporean filmmaker to have her student short selected by the Venice Film Festival in 2002, and she has also been selected for the Berlinale Talent Campus (2009), Torino FilmLab (2010), and Taipei Golden Horse Film Academy (2010), the latter led by Hou Hsiao-Hsien. Yet the work accomplished within minor networks that exists alongside these major accolades is not to be dismissed as trivial or marginal. Minor networks allow filmmakers from emergent, smaller film industries in Asia to negotiate restrictive national cinema frameworks and to create transnational connections that cross commercial as well as geographical boundaries. For instance, although Koh's career received a boost after the Rotterdam commission of *Dirty Bitch*, she continues to make minor works in collaboration with other women filmmakers while developing her first feature film.

Active ties among women filmmakers in Asian cinema, though nascent, are already building new opportunities and potentials beyond the dominant auteurism that accompanies feature film accolades at major international film festivals. Short films allow for a rethinking of authorship as part of the varied terrain of women's film culture in Asia and amid the uncertainty of the commercial landscape of global filmmaking.

Conclusion

I have argued that in order to account for the participation of women filmmakers in contemporary Asian cinema using the short film form, we need to recognize in-betweenness in the forms in which these filmmakers work as well as the strategies they employ as a matter of survival and a means of visibility. As a key example of the mode of in-betweenness in which Asian women filmmakers operate, Koh's *Dirty Bitch* reinterprets certain themes, symbols, and techniques not only from the Denis film that inspired it but also across a minor-to-minor transnational circuit of women's filmmaking and queer Asian cinema. The symbolism of the rabbit employed in Koh's version produces an entirely different—and queer—connotation in the context of Chinese same-sex cultures than it does in Denis's film. Similarly, the use of the male voice-over, which appears in both *Nénette et Boni* and *Dirty Bitch*, is reinterpreted in the latter in the form of a Chinese woman lip-synching to a French rap song, resulting in a completely altered political and enunciative act. Meanwhile, in Koh's exquisite corpse projects, authorship is reconfigured through an ethic of collaboration, a form of collective enunciation that is as much local as it is transnational.

I do not intend to participate in a debate about Eastern collectivism versus so-called Western individualism. Rather, I wish to emphasize how short films like *Dirty Bitch* and the segments of the omnibus projects discussed engage strategies of both national and transnational connection. Although it is important to remain mindful of the local specificities to gendered and sexual identities, there is also value in considering regional solidarities among women filmmakers in Asia.[41] Women in Asia are actively working not only, or not predominantly, within the feature film industry but also within a range of other, minor modes of production. Moreover, they are collaborating transnationally, in political as well as aesthetic terms, from inception and production to circulation, distribution, and exhibition. It is thus important to consider the minor transnational networks in which women's filmmaking in Asia exists beyond its national contexts, particularly as it is women's work that foregrounds the minor transnational circuits of queer Asian cinema and the double exclusion of women's queer cinema from the feature film and auteurist terrains of international art cinema. Queer film scenes in Asia are generally too small for us to think of them solely in terms of their local or national contexts, or indeed only in terms of feature films.[42]

The cultural value associated with making a feature film continues to marginalize short film production, positioning the latter outside the realm of traditional authorship. It is thus necessary to find an analytical frame that can account for and value this minor form both in terms of reading practices and as a mode of authorship. I have sought to do so in my reading of *Dirty Bitch* by placing it within a minor transnational network of women's filmmaking and queer culture in Asia.

It is promising that access to short films from Asia continues to grow via a range of alternative modes of distribution and exhibition. Beyond the various festival circuits, short films are increasingly being distributed via nontheatrical means, including video-sharing sites, such as YouTube and Vimeo, and Internet fan sites.[43] Singaporean start-up company Viddsee, an online social viewing platform for Southeast Asian short films, has grown a subscription base of over 60,000 since it was launched in January 2013. Alternate channels like these are creating further possibilities for short-format works to circulate and be consumed across borders. In the context of Asian cinema's growing regionalization and the consolidation of inter-Asian circuits of production, distribution, exhibition, and reception, it is increasingly important to consider how changing notions of authorship are affecting women's filmmaking and in particular to make visible the minor transnational circuits that function in between dominant modes of authorship.

Notes

I would like to thank the participants of "Between Worlds: The Place of the Female Director in Twenty-First-Century Film Cultures and Feminist Theory," a workshop held in November 2011 at Monash University, where a very early draft of this article was presented. I am indebted to the workshop organizers, Therese Davis and Belinda Smaill, for their invaluable advice during the revision of this essay, and especially to Patty White for her insight, generosity, and intellect. Thanks also to Sun Koh for giving me access to her wonderful films.

1. Lingzhen Wang, introduction to *Chinese Women's Cinema: Transnational Contexts*, ed. Lingzhen Wang (New York: Columbia University Press, 2011), 22.

2. Jan Uhde and Yvonne Ng Uhde, "Singapore Cinema: Spotlight on Short Film Production," *Spectator* 24, no. 2 (2004): 18.

3. The Singapore Film Commission's now defunct Short Film Grant supported over seventy short films in 2006, compared to only eleven short films in 1998. The definition of a short film for the purposes of the grant was any film under thirty minutes. In September 2011 Singapore's Media Development Authority overhauled its grants schemes, replacing them with five new schemes covering development, production, marketing, and talent assistance. Short films will now be funded under one of these schemes.

4. Nick Deocampo, *Short Film: Emergence of a New Philippine Cinema* (Manila: Communication Foundation for Asia, 1985), 1. Emphasis in original.

5. Uhde and Uhde, "Singapore Cinema," 20.

6. Each of these filmmakers has made at least one film (feature length or short) with homosexual characters and/or themes. See Royston Tan's short film *Anniversary* (2009), Loo Zi-han's *Solos* (2007), and Boo Junfeng's *Tanjong Rhu* (2009).

7. Roy Tan, "Singapore Gay Films," sgWiki, sgwiki.com/wiki/Singapore_gay_films (accessed July 2013). In 2010 Sun Koh's *Dirty Bitch* won the best director and best fiction awards at the inaugural Singapore Short Film Awards.

8. Juan Foo, "Mini Cinema," FilmsAsia, December 2002, filmsasia.net/gpage77.html. Evidence of an emerging minor transnational network of Asian short films can be seen in regional initiatives such as the Asian Short Film Awards, the online distribution platform for Southeast Asian cinema Viddsee, and the archiving of regional (especially Southeast Asian) short films in the Asian Film Archive, Singapore.

9. Deocampo, *Short Film*, viii.

10. Gilles Deleuze and Félix Guattari, *Kafka: Toward a Minor Literature*, trans. Dana Polan (1975; Minneapolis: University of Minnesota Press, 1986); Tom Gunning, "Toward a Minor Cinema," *Motion Picture* 3, nos. 1–2 (1989–90): 2–5.

11. Gunning, "Toward a Minor Cinema," 3.

12. Alison Butler, *Women's Cinema: The Contested Screen* (London: Wallflower, 2002); Patricia White, "Lesbian Minor Cinema," *Screen* 49, no. 4 (2008): 410–25.

13. Butler, *Women's Cinema*, 19. Deleuze writes, "Because the people are missing, the author is in a situation of producing utterances which are already collective, which are like the seeds of people to come." Gilles Deleuze, *Cinema 2: The Time-Image*, trans. Hugh Tomlinson and Robert Galeta (London: Athlone, 1989), 221.

14. White, "Lesbian Minor Cinema," 413.

15. Helen Hok-Sze Leung, "Queer Asian Cinemas," in *The Bent Lens: A World Guide to Gay and Lesbian Film*, ed. Lisa Daniel and Claire Jackson (New York: Alyson, 2003), 14. Leung argues that outside the festival circuit it is "difficult to speak of the influence of these films as though they form a coherent body of work. The very notion of a 'queer Asian cinema' is in many ways a festival invention" (14).

16. Butler, *Women's Cinema*, 119.

17. Will Higbee and Song Hwee Lim, "Concepts of Transnational Cinema: Towards a Critical Transnationalism in Film Studies," *Transnational Cinemas* 1, no. 1 (2010): 15.

18. Wang, introduction to Wang, *Chinese Women's Cinema*, 2.

19. Nicola Spakowski, "'Gender' Trouble: Feminism in China under the Impact of Western Theory and the Spatialization of Identity," *positions* 19, no. 1 (2011): 31–54.

20. Chandra Talpade Mohanty, "Cartographies of Struggle: Third World Women and the Politics of Feminism," in *Third World Women and the Politics of Feminism*, ed. Chandra Talpade Mohanty, Ann Russo, and Lourdes Torres (Bloomington: Indiana University Press, 1991), 4.

21. See note 42 for evidence of the regional development of (queer) women's filmmaking in Asia.

22. Françoise Lionnet and Shu-mei Shih, introduction to *Minor Transnationalism*, ed. Françoise Lionnet and Shu-mei Shih (Durham, NC: Duke University Press, 2005), 7.

23. Koh states that she was commissioned for this work because "the programmers thought I was a suitable candidate, being a woman and a wild one at that." "Production Talk: *Dirty Bitch* by Sun Koh," *SINdie*, 2 March 2009, www.sindie.sg/2009/03/production-talk-dirty-bitch-by-sun-koh.html.

24. Sun Koh, "Filmography," sunkoh.com/#!filmography (accessed July 2013).

25. Helen Hok-Sze Leung, "Queerscapes in Contemporary Hong Kong Cinema," *positions* 9, no. 2 (2001): 426.

26. Helen Hok-Sze Leung, *Undercurrents: Queer Culture and Postcolonial Hong Kong* (Hong Kong: Hong Kong University Press, 2008), 2.

27. Wenqing Kang, *Obsession: Male Same-Sex Relations in China, 1900–1950* (Hong Kong: Hong Kong University Press, 2009), 37–38.

28. Michael Szonyi, "The Cult of Hu Tianbao and the Eighteenth-Century Discourse of Homosexuality," *Late Imperial China* 19, no. 1 (1998): 1–25.

29. To this day, same-sex couples visit this temple to pray for love.

30. For a theory of texts' pervasive queerness in the absence of overt homosexuality, see Alexander Doty, *Making Things Perfectly Queer: Interpreting Mass Culture* (Minneapolis: University of Minnesota Press, 1993), xii.

31. Teresa de Lauretis, "Queer Texts, Bad Habits, and the Issue of a Future," *GLQ* 17, no. 2 (2011): 244.

32. The Kewpie doll is based on Rose O'Neill's 1909 illustrations for *Ladies' Home Journal*. First produced in Germany (made out of bisque and celluloid, and later hard plastic), the dolls are popular not only in Europe and America but also in Asia, especially Japan, where they exist within local *kawaii* (cute) culture.

33. Lee Edelman, *No Future: Queer Theory and the Death Drive* (Durham, NC: Duke University Press, 2004), 4.

34. José Esteban Muñoz, *Cruising Utopia: The Then and There of Queer Futurity* (New York: New York University Press, 2009), 11.

35. Koh has said that *Dirty Bitch* is a response to "censorship and the hidden humour of Claire Denis" ("Production Talk"). Elsewhere, she has described the film as a "love letter" to Singapore's censors (Koh, "Filmography").

36. Zee, "Sun Shines on Singapore Queer Cinema," *Fridae*, 26 March 2008, fridae.asia/newsfeatures/2008/03/26/2026.sun-shines-on-singapore-queer-cinema. "Exquisite corpse" is a Surrealist parlor game.

37. "*Sweden 7/Sverige 7*," FundedByMe, www.fundedbyme.com/en/campaign/395/sweden-7-sverige-7/ (accessed July 2013).

38. Zee, "Sun Shines on Singapore Queer Cinema."

39. "*Sweden 7/Sverige 7*."

40. In addition to the collaborative works already discussed, another example of a transnational collaborative film featuring the participation of women filmmakers from both within and outside Asia is *Children of Srikandi* (*Anak-Anak Srikandi*, 2012). An Indonesian-German-Swiss coproduction directed by the Children of Srikandi Collective and produced by Laura Coppens and Angelika Levi, *Children of Srikandi* blends documentary,

fiction, and experimental elements. The film began as a workshop that led to a collaborative film project reflecting the directors' lived experiences as queer women in Indonesia. Participants worked on each other's films as crew members or actresses. Collaborative projects like this one effectively create a feature film out of a number of collaborative shorts, redefining the meaning of authorship to incorporate emerging forms of transnational solidarity.

41. Megan Sinnott, "Borders, Diaspora, and Regional Connections: Trends in Asian 'Queer' Studies," *Journal of Asian Studies* 69, no. 1 (2010): 18.

42. To provide a sense of the size of the national queer film scenes within Asia, the following list is a survey of feature-length productions (productions with running times of at least sixty minutes) with lesbian main characters made by women directors in Asia since 2000:

    China: *The Box* (*He zi*, dir. Ying Weiwei, 2001) (documentary), *Fish and Elephant* (*Yu he Daxiang*, dir. Li Yu, 2002), *Lost in You* (*Lalala*, dir. Zhu Yiye, 2006), *Love Mime* (*Xiaoshu de xiatian*, dir. Zhu Yiye, 2008)

    Hong Kong: *Ho Yuk: Let's Love Hong Kong* (dir. Yau Ching, 2002), *Butterfly* (*Hu Die*, dir. Yan Yan Mak, 2004)

    Indonesia: *Children of Srikandi* (documentary/fiction hybrid)

    Japan: *Love/Juice* (dir. Kaze Shindo, 2000), *Sugar Sweet* (dir. Desiree Lim, 2001)

    Singapore: *Women Who Love Women: Conversations in Singapore* (dir. Lim Mayling, 2008) (documentary)

    Taiwan: *Corners* (*Si Jiao-Luo*, dir. Zero Chou and Hoho Liu, 2001), *Incidental Journey* (*Haijiao tianya*, dir. Chen Jofei, 2002), *Love Me, If You Can* (*Fei yue qin hai*, dir. Alice Wang, 2003), *Love's Lone Flower* (*Gu Lian Hua*, dir. Tsao Jui-Yuan, 2005), *Spider Lilies* (*Ci qing*, dir. Zero Chou, 2007), *Drifting Flowers* (*Piao lang qing chun*, dir. Zero Chou, 2008)

    Thailand: *Yes or No? So, I Love You* (*Yak Rak Ko Rak Loei*, dir. Sarasawadee Wongsompetch, 2009), *She: Their Love Story* (*Ruang Rak Rawang Ther*, dir. Sranya Noithai, 2012)

    I have tried to be as exhaustive as possible in constructing this list but may have missed some titles. If the list were to include lesbian-themed films directed by men it would be much longer. Not all of the directors listed are queer, although several are.

43. In an example from public broadcast television, online replays of *Daughters of Club Bilitis*, an hour-long Korean Broadcasting System drama about three generations of lesbian couples, were pulled due to public pressure three days after the drama aired in August 2011. Charles Junwoo Park, "Lesbians in Drama Test Society's Limits," Han Cinema, 18 August 2011, hancinema.net /lesbians-in-drama-test-society-s-limits-32357.html. Full-length clips have since circulated online in a variety of subtitled forms produced by fans. The circulation of queer films with subtitling is limited. Dedicated fans will often provide translations and subtitles for texts, anticipating transnational audiences.

Olivia Khoo is a senior lecturer in film and television studies at Monash University. She is author of *The Chinese Exotic: Modern Diasporic Femininity* (Hong Kong University Press, 2007); coauthor, with Belinda Smaill and Audrey Yue, of *Transnational Australian Cinema: Ethics in the Asian Diasporas* (Lexington, 2013); and coeditor, with Sean Metzger, of *Futures of Chinese Cinema: Technologies and Temporalities in Chinese Screen Cultures* (Intellect, 2009) and, with Audrey Yue, of *Sinophone Cinemas* (Palgrave Macmillan, 2014).

Figure 5. The Singapore Merlion spits out Kewpie dolls as Zhen (Serene Chen) runs away. *Dirty Bitch*

Figure 1. *Everybody Dies but Me* (*Vse umrut, a ya ostanus*, dir. Valeria Gai Germanika, Russia, 2008)

"Becoming-Girl" in the New Russian Cinema: Youth and Valeria Gai Germanika's Films and Television

Julia Vassilieva

When five members of Pussy Riot, a Russian feminist punk rock protest group, staged a performance in Moscow's Cathedral of Christ the Savior on 12 February 2012, the world was offered a rare glimpse of radical feminist youth culture in postcommunist Russia. Three members of the group were arrested and jailed for two years in the aftermath of the event. While their performance was specifically designed as a protest against the alliance between the Russian Orthodox Church and the current government, the group's broader agenda encompasses democracy, feminism, and LGBT rights in contemporary Russia. Yet as Vikki Turbine notes, "while [Pussy Riot's] feminism is often mentioned in international coverage, it is rarely the subject of serious analysis and further consideration of how it can be viewed as particularly radical and oppositional in the context of contemporary Russian gender politics, where hostility to feminism and a regression of *women's* human [*sic*] is evident."[1] The serious analysis Turbine refers to is also absent from discussions of contemporary Russian cinema, despite the fact that female voices are increasingly important to this cinema. Less known in the West than Pussy Riot, but part of the same generation, is the female director Valeria Gai Germanika, born in 1984, who has been the subject of controversy but who has also achieved unprecedented success in Russia. This essay focuses on her output, which, like that of Pussy Riot, gives voice to women and youth. While her work is frequently described as controversial, little effort has been made to theorize, or indeed to understand, her oeuvre.

Germanika's work casts light on the contemporary terrain of Russian filmmaking and its relationship to Russian youth, who find themselves caught between the communist past and the postcommunist future. Her public profile has emerged over the last ten years with documentary shorts such as *Sisters* (*Syostry*, 2005), *Girls* (*Devochki*, 2005), and *Boys* (*Malchiki*, 2007) and the sixty-part TV series *School* (*Shkola*, Channel One Russia, 2010). This body of work deals with issues that face contemporary Russian youth and is so confrontational that it has been the subject of a special debate in the Russian parliament (Duma). Consequently, Germanika has become visible as an auteur who operates simultaneously within several historical, conceptual, and industrial formations: she is a female director in a male-dominated post-Soviet cinema industry; an independent director in a production landscape defined by large studios; and, most important, a young director articulating the perspective of youth in a cultural milieu traditionally dominated by the views of older generations. Her work and profile as a director thus offer a specifically gendered and generational dimension to the ways in which geopolitics inflects popular culture in postcommunist Eastern Europe.

My essay outlines the context of Germanika's output and explores how discourses of femininity and adolescence intersect in her film and television work. Specifically, the essay engages with her feature *Everybody Dies but Me* (*Vse umrut, a ya ostanus*, 2008) and the series *School* and addresses the issue of subject positioning raised by her work. I suggest that in the context of Russia's postcommunist transition, Germanika's work not only valorizes a female perspective and delivers a critique of the dominant male subject of Soviet cultural production and politics but also offers a new way to imagine subjectivity through its figuration of youth as a site of change. I mobilize Gilles Deleuze and Félix Guattari's concept of *becoming-girl* to argue that youth and femininity emerge in her work not as the other side of the male subject of communism but as another order of representation.

Valeria Gai Germanika: A Woman Filmmaker between Worlds

Germanika made her cinematic debut soon after the turn of the twenty-first century and as part of a generation of young female filmmakers in Russia that includes Oksana Bichkova (*Piter FM*, 2006), Anna Melikian (*Mermaid* [*Rusalka*, 2007]), and Angelina Nikonova (*Twilight Portrait* [*Portret v sumerkakh*, 2011]). Working within the male-dominated Russian film industry, these young female directors often follow production, distribution, and exhibition routes that are characteristic of low-budget film and television production, such as arthouse and festival circuits.[2] While these young auteurs often display an interest in women's issues and perspectives, Germanika is distinctive. Her work is marked by an uncompromising realism that, in the context of Russia's post-communist transition, has added urgency to her output. Questions of truth and the real have been central to political, cultural, and philosophical debates since the collapse of communism. With autobiographical motifs and a focus on teenagers and young women, Germanika produces a compassionate cinema of witnessing that represents a new perspective in Russian cinema. The way Germanika treats youth is radically different from Soviet cinema of the communist era and cinema produced during the 1990s, a period characterized by the large-scale reforms of perestroika.

"Youth film" has existed in Soviet cinema since its early days—for instance, Nikolai Ekk's famous 1931 film *Road to Life* (*Putyovka v zhizn*). During the Soviet era the youth wing of the Communist Party, the Komsomol, imposed a model of "idealistic youth marching purposefully along the golden road to socialism, untrammeled by the vices of their capitalist counterparts."[3] During perestroika, the rejection of socialist values and lifestyle became evident in a whole range of pursuits such as the formation of youth gangs, a sudden and widespread experimentation with drugs (which had been previously unavailable in the USSR), and changes in the expression of sexual behavior, all of which became urgent social concerns for the new era. Youth films of the early perestroika era explored intergenerational conflict, addressed growing concern over the sexual profligacy of the young, and focused on the alienation of youth. These themes were poignantly reflected in the film titles of the era such as *Is It Easy to Be Young?* (*Vai viegli būt jaunam?/Legko li bit molodim?*, 1987) by Latvian director Yuris Podnieks and Georgi Gavrilov's *Confession: A Chronicle of Alienation* (*Ispoved: Kronika otchuzdeniya*, 1989).

While these films represented rich and diverse engagements with emerging youth culture, they were lacking in one important respect: they were all made from a socially normative point of view located outside the youth world and were often judgmental and didactic. While the approaches in these films ranged from descriptive to analytical, and some attempted to suggest that society bore a measure of responsibility for problems concerning youth, they ultimately aimed at delivering a verdict. As Hilary Pilkington notes, "The cultural practice of young people in the perestroika period was read above all politically, and a struggle was waged to 'win back' and 'channel' youthful energies into a party-led program for the revitalization of Soviet society."[4] These efforts soon came to an end amid the total collapse of the Soviet system. As Pilkington further observes, "It was then that the dominant image of youth as constructors of the bright (communist) future was replaced by that of young people as a lost generation with neither past nor future" (201). The beginning of the twenty-first century ushered in an era of relative political and social stability in Russia. This was accompanied, however, by "a fading of optimism concerning any clearly defined, near-at-hand goals for social transformation."[5] Some theorists argued that "the post-Soviet" was not appropriate terminology. The discursive rendering of the transitional period had overwhelmingly shifted from rupture to continuity. It was in this politico-historical context that Germanika entered the Russian cultural scene.

Germanika trained at the Internews Cinema and Television

School and started directing at the age of nineteen. Her first documentary, *Sisters,* received the Grand Prix in the Shorts Competition at Kinotavr, the most prestigious film festival in Russia, while her first feature, *Everybody Dies but Me,* brought her international recognition with two prizes at the Cannes International Film Festival (the Caméra d'Or jury's Special Mention and the Critics' Week youth prize). Most recently, she has achieved nationwide exposure in her homeland with *School* and *A Short Course on How to Live a Happy Life* (*Kratkiy kurs schaslivoy zhini,* Channel One Russia, 2012). As the titles of Germanika's films amply demonstrate, she focuses on youth and often specifically on the experiences of girls and young women. The subjects of her work are adolescents and young adults in states of simultaneous becoming and entrapment, attesting to both the intrinsic vitality and potentiality of youth and the dysfunctional effects of the old Soviet system's remnants, which still deeply penetrate the fabric of contemporary Russian society.

Germanika's early documentary shorts established the themes, style, and relationship with her subjects that characterize her oeuvre. These films, which Germanika shot herself using MiniDV, focus on the everyday experiences of teenagers in Moscow's remote suburb of Strogino, where the director grew up. Suburbs like this have become synonymous with the strata of contemporary Russian society for whom perestroika was not about expanding options but about shattering hopes for the future. These permanently marginalized ordinary Russians are distinctly different from the emergent Russian middle class or oligarchs, the super-rich elite in whose hands the nation's wealth has become concentrated. While not focusing specifically on issues of inequality, Germanika delivers an insider, cinema vérité–style perspective on the daily functioning of this universe. She follows the quotidian movements of her teenage protagonists: having lengthy conversations on ubiquitous landings, smoking and drinking, dressing up, applying makeup, doing hair, and self-piercing. She occupies the position of a friend sharing these experiences rather than that of investigator. In these films Germanika's own position as a young woman and a rebellious cult figure epitomizing countercultural development in Russia overlaps complexly with the identities of her subjects. In this way her films are reminiscent of early feminist documentaries in which, as Julia Lesage poignantly writes, "no woman is filmed as an object; everyone is a subject."[6]

Unlike filmmakers of the previous generation, who addressed youth issues in Russian cinema from an external position, Germanika positions herself inside the world that she films. Her early documentaries focus on teenagers and were made when she was just emerging from her own teenage years; she films her own generation and speaks for them and to them. This marks a radical break with the dominant discourse on youth in postsocialist cultures, where, as Anikó Imre notes, " 'Youth film,' in the sense of a genre of films that *address* young people, is at best an emerging concept."[7]

"Life Caught Unawares": Observing Youth Culture

Everybody Dies but Me builds on the themes of Germanika's earlier work, focusing on three schoolgirls: Katya (Polina Filonenko), Vika (Olga Shuvalova), and Zhanna (Agnia Kusnetsova).[8] The three girls are in year nine and approximately fourteen years old. Katya, Vika, and Zhanna can be understood through Deleuze and Guattari's notion of *becoming-girl*, an argument I will develop below. First I attend to the narrative structure of *Everybody Dies but Me*, the relation between this film and the teen film genre, the film's specific setting and temporality, and the symbolism of the title.

The film's narrative covers five days in the lives of students attending a suburban Moscow high school. During this short period the three protagonists go through a variety of events, the dramatic nature of which is offset by the banality and casualness of their rendering. These events include the students arguing with parents and running away from home, having their first sexual experiences, experimenting with drugs and alcohol, self-harming, fighting with peers, and having conflicts with teachers, to name a few. This multifaceted representation of teenagers contains elements of the three broad discursive categories that, according to Catherine Driscoll, characterize the teen film in the West: teen as problem, teen as institution, and youth as party.[9] *Everybody Dies but Me* indicates the emergence of Western teen cultural sensibilities in postcommunist

Russia. However, the film does not fit the generic classification of teen film and also resists rigid classification of any kind: its themes, narrative, and characters are deliberately nonformulaic. While narrative and stylistic practices of the teen film genre tend to generalize youth experience, Germanika's approach individualizes. *Everybody Dies but Me* raises the question of what it means to grow up as a girl in contemporary Russia. To answer it, Germanika engages with contemporary Russian social complexities, constructing situations and characters that are unique and localized.

Everybody Dies but Me polarized Russian audiences. Some praised it for its uncompromised authenticity in representing a generational conflict, for recreating the organic world of a contemporary Moscow suburb, and for being lifelike and steeped in the personal experience of contemporary teens. Others attacked it for its sensationalist representation of Russian youth. Indeed, this criticism escalated to moral panic in 2010 with the release of Germanika's next project, *School*, ultimately leading to highly politicized debates in the Russian parliament that caused the show to be taken off the air temporarily. A number of politicians, pundits, and representatives of various educational bodies denounced what they saw as Germanika's excessively dark representation of teen life and the school system. Her works were seen as contributing to the moral degeneration of youth and as detrimental to national pride.[10]

However, neither *Everybody Dies but Me* nor *School* participates in *chernukha*, a slang term derived from the root *chern-* or "black" that came to describe the 1990s trend that brought to the screen all of Soviet society's previously suppressed ills and sins amid the newly gained freedom of glasnost and perestroika.[11] Chernukha exposed problems that had plagued Soviet society for years with representational attitudes ranging from self-lacerating to exploitative. This tendency toward exposure was epitomized in *Little Vera* (*Malenkaya Vera*, dir. Vasili Pichul, Soviet Union, 1988), a film that sensationalizes sex and violence. In an attempt to denigrate *Everybody Dies but Me*, one Russian critic suggested that the film looks like what *Little Vera* would have looked like if its eponymous protagonist had made it herself.[12] Indeed, the change of perspective identified by this critic is what differentiates Germanika's work most profoundly from the other teen films. She "sees each of three heroines from the point of view of a peer, understanding and deciphering each detail for spectators of a different age group, who have a different view on life."[13] Germanika focuses intently on the three girls at the center of the film: much of the film consists of close-ups of their faces and their movements, which the camera follows in jerky tracking shots. Germanika creates the palpable impression that there is someone else in the scene, someone who is intimately familiar with what is happening and who, moreover, is allowed to be there. The camerawork by celebrated cinematographer Alisher Hamidchodjaev creates for the viewer a distinct feeling of "being-with" a character. As Teresa Rizzo notes, a cinematic sense of being-with a character "opens up a way of thinking about subjectivity as occurring with others rather than against another."[14] Mobilizing this proximity, Germanika creates the conditions for this new form of subjectivity to emerge in her film.

Germanika's valorization of observation can be related to her background as a documentary filmmaker and association with the indie Kinoteatr.doc, a contemporary avant-garde group that supports and promotes young documentary filmmakers and is "interested in real life and cinema that relates to it."[15] There are notable similarities between Germanika's style and the principles of Dogme 95, specifically in the pursuit of veracity and authenticity. Germanika adopts many formal devices of Dogme, such as a handheld camera, natural locations and light, and minimal use of nondiegetic music. She also produces a reality effect through her use of conventions associated with such media forms as camcorder footage, home movies, and video diaries. In this context, Germanika's approach is often compared to Dziga Vertov's intention to record "life as it is," to grasp reality as it unfolds. As Aleksandr Kolbovskii notes:

Gai-Germanika's past as documentary filmmaker transpires like a photo in the process of being developed. *Everybody Dies but Me* possesses the unconditional accuracy and reliability of a document, recording a certain cross-section of the generation and the personal attitudes within this generation. Moreover, it provides an exact enough and sharp picture of modern Russian reality. So, in this case we are dealing with artistic-documentary cinema, if by artistic we understand the skill to recreate reality through fiction films and a degree of authorial judgment of reality, and if we understand by documentation authenticity, reality, truth.[16]

Like Germanika's previous documentary projects, *Everybody Dies but Me* is set against the bleak backdrop of the Moscow suburbs, where life seems to be in limbo between communism and postcommunism. The setting diverges from the long tradition of representing Moscow in a romantic or glamorous light, as epitomized by Soviet films of the fifties and now enthusiastically recycled with a sense of nostalgia by the current wave of Russian cinema. For example, *Lucky Trouble* (*Vykrutasy*, dir. Levan Gabriadze, 2011), a mainstream Russian comedy, refers extensively to earlier films set in Moscow such as *Walking the Streets of Moscow* (*Ya shagayu po Moskve*, dir. Georgiy Daneliya, 1964) and *Tanya* (*Svetlyy Put*, dir. Grigori Alexandrov, 1940). In this mode, Moscow's iconic landmarks, and specifically the art deco high-rises built during the Stalin era, are used as points of reference for the solid heroic past, which in turn provides a basis for a solid and heroic future. In contrast to this cinematic Moscow, Germanika sets her film in an anonymous, dilapidated block of flats built in the 1980s, neglected parks, and intricate labyrinths formed by rusty garages and workshops. The cinematic topography of *Everybody Dies but Me* confirms Lily Avrutin's suggestion that "an artistic model capable of arriving at new meanings . . . represents not a forward movement along a straight road—as in traditional narrative—but a wandering, roaming exploration in a space of collage, where the labyrinth of closed time-space is the most suitable chronotope for searching out new post-totalitarian meanings."[17] Shooting on location, Germanika uses real dwelling spaces and their dated, claustrophobic interiors to depict a form of city space where time seems to be static, weighed down by its Soviet past. Its inhabitants live here one day at a time, often without work and seemingly with only one option to distract themselves—cheap alcohol sold in makeshift shops. Within this fossilized and anonymous terrain, however, the film introduces its own fluid spatiality, mirroring the constant, complex movements of its teen protagonists.

The setting of *Everybody Dies but Me* resonates with its title, which indicates that the work engages not only with teen culture but also with issues of life and death. The film is bookended symbolically by almost identical scenes of two funeral repasts that take place in Katya's home: one held on the day of her grandmother's funeral, the other on the ninth day after her grandmother's death when, according to Russian tradition, relatives and friends gather to pray for the soul of the deceased. This juxtaposition of intense teen longing for pleasure—exemplified by the five-day wait for the disco that structures the film's duration—and the presence of the powerful death motif implies that life itself is at risk: everything is fragile, and youth is precariously positioned between becoming and annihilation.

The importance to Germanika of the opposition of life and death is later confirmed in *School*, in which death through illness, suicide, or accident features prominently over the series's sixty episodes. The narrative of *School* begins with the near-death experience of the elderly headmaster, one of the protagonists. His heart attack and subsequent months-long balance between life and death indicate the demise of patriarchy, the older generation, and the exhausted ideological system of the Soviet era and usher in disintegration across the headmaster's family and school. The repeatedly foregrounded motif of the disintegration of adulthood's normative world significantly reconfigures one of the main tropes of both Russian and Western teen films: the expectation that the troubled teen will eventually enter the stable world of adulthood. As Jon Lewis observes, if in many teen films the teenagers "focus on a single concern: the breakdown of traditional forms of authority; patriarchy; law and order; and institutions like the school, the church, and the family," the narrative resolution always entails "the eventual discovery of viable and often traditional forms of authority."[18] The distinctiveness of Germanika's approach is that such resolution is not only denied, it is figured as being impossible in principle.

Germanika depicts both the public sphere of school and the private sphere of family in states of crisis. The school system, central to teenagers' socialization and a key instrument in forging future citizens, clings desperately to power. The school tries to mobilize fear as its primary strategy of control. This is staged in the mise-en-scène of the opening sequence, in which shot composition and rhythm work to create a metaphor of school as a prison. However, the school's prestige and importance are continuously undermined by the utter indifference and lack of respect of its charges.

Before this theme of disintegration emerged fully in *School, Everybody Dies but Me* mirrored the antagonism between resentful youth and the school as repressive institution through powerfully staged generational conflict between parents and children. In the film, parents are spatially separated from children; their characters are rendered simply and offered much less screen time, posing them in opposition to the younger generation. Katya's parents are a good example of this tendency: her father, unemployed and spending his days lying on the couch, stands as a symbol of the middle-aged man in Russia who has not caught up with the post-Soviet reality, while her mother, working long hours at an unspecified job, is exhausted and defeated. Katya's father asserts his authority by victimizing his daughter, often using brutal physical violence, while her mother watches with a mixture of indifference and acceptance. Katya's reaction to her parents' disciplinary methods demonstrates poignantly the depth of the gulf that separates the generations. A close-up of Katya's face when she is hopelessly trying to protect herself from a senseless beating by her father, like the close-up of Antoine Doinel's face in François Truffaut's *The 400 Blows* (*Les quatre cents coups*, France, 1959), floods the screen with the pain of the weak, powerless, misunderstood, and ignored, begging the unspoken question why. However, as Germanika's film unfolds, it makes clear that the older generation has little real effect on the life of the younger one; the institutions of parenting and the school system are cadavers of the old system and do not provide any firm basis or value system for progress. In the last scene of the film, Katya, who has been beaten up by her peers, returns home covered in blood and with tears streaming down her face. She says defiantly, "Everybody dies but me." The scene strikes a compelling balance between a rejection of the old and teenage megalomania—she has suffered and paid for this affirmation of belief in her future.

The Multivoiced World of *School*

School aired in 2010 on Channel One, Russia's primary state broadcaster. An example of televisual long-form narrative, *School* represents a novelistic mode of storytelling.[19] Complex narrative arcs and an extended ensemble cast create an impression of considerable density and lifelikeness. *School* features more than fifty characters and comprises more than ten narrative threads, creating a polyphonic world characterized by a multitude of perspectives. In a style that mirrors the features that Mikhail Bakhtin identified in Fyodor Dostoyevsky's novels, *School* features a plurality of consciousnesses in place of an omniscient narrator. This plurality is achieved not only through the narrative but also through Germanika's approach to cinematography, which creates a decentered gaze. There is a noticeable lack of establishing, reestablishing, and objective shots. Following the complex trajectories of its multiple protagonists, the footage consists almost entirely of point-of-view shots, without privileging any single perspective.

While it has been argued that *School* delivers an in-depth systemic exploration of failing moral values, corruption, nationalism, and greed in the educational sector in modern Russia, in my view its overriding interest lies in the depiction of conflicts of identity that threaten and destabilize any sense of personal coherence and continuity. What emerges is a model of identity as flexible, fragmented, and elusive. Two student characters introduced at the beginning of the series, Ania Nosova (Valentina Lukashchuk) and Ilía Epifanov (Aleksei Litvinenko), provide a good illustration of this protean model of identity. Ania has been studying at home for the previous two years due to illness. Both of her parents are absent and she has been raised under the overbearing care of her grandfather, who is also headmaster at the school. She is desperate to return to school to escape this suffocating domestic world and renew her social life. When she does, however, a chain of misunderstandings leads to her rejection by schoolmates. Tragically, her efforts to connect to people only lead to her greater alienation and isolation. Ania follows a downward spiral ending with her suicide—by taking drugs prescribed to her grandmother—in one of the final episodes.

Ania's emotional conflicts epitomize those of the characters in *School*. Needy, fragile, loving, and tender in some situations and cold, indifferent, bitter, and rejecting in others, Ania is capable of acts of manipulation and betrayal (she falsely accuses one of the teachers of sexually abusing her), but also of loyalty and compassion (particularly evident in her care for her paralyzed, dying grandfather). The fluidity of her character is also apparent in the visual transformations that she undergoes during the series. While initially Ania is presented as demure, this characterization is subverted when she places photos of her naked body on the Internet and takes on the appearance of an "emo" girl, coloring her hair black and applying exaggerated makeup. Ania's tendency to reconfigure herself is further evident in her extensive use of social media, as she presents herself under different names and posts fictitious stories about herself.

Ilía, the second core character, is presented as contradictory, brittle, and chameleonlike. In the absence of his father, Ilía accepts responsibility for his terminally ill mother, who struggles with cancer throughout the series and dies in episode 52. He looks after her on a daily basis, organizing an operation and earning income by selling dietary supplements and cleaning apartments. Yet while Ilía is caring and protective toward his mother, he readily shows a brutal and indifferent side to other people—including his classmates, teachers, and other relatives—and is not above stealing or engaging in blackmail.

It is impossible to place Germanika's characters in definite moral or ethical categories. As Hubert J. M. Hermans and Harry J. G. Kempen note, Bakhtinian polyphony enables "one and the same individual to live in a multiplicity of worlds with each world having its own author telling a story relatively independent of the authors of the other worlds."[20] Not only is the story world of the series composed of a multiplicity of voices associated with each of the protagonists, but each protagonist, in turn, contains within him- or herself a variety of often incompatible personae.

This radical instability of identity can be read not only narratologically but also from a sociological and psychological perspective. Zygmunt Bauman argues that in the postmodern world our sociopolitical, cultural, professional, religious, and sexual identities are undergoing a process of continual transformation and becoming increasingly "liquid." In a globalized world of rapid change, our identities are in a state of continuous flux.[21] From this perspective the liquid character of self, identity, and subjectivity embodied in Germanika's protagonists can be read symptomatically as indicating Russia's entry into the postmodern world of late capitalism. Germanika places her teen protagonists' liquid sense of identity in contrast to their "solid" environment, primarily exemplified by two settings: the school and their family homes. If the school provides a clinical, depersonalized space, the family apartments are often overcrowded with mismatched furniture and insignificant objects. Both of these settings create stifling environments in which the movements of both the characters and the camera are restricted and overly controlled.

There is, however, one important departure from this restriction that is apparent in the mise-en-scène and employed extensively by Germanika in both *School* and *Everybody Dies but Me* (as well as in *Girls*): staircases and landings. In *School*, these sites are favorite backdrops for the teen protagonists as they hang out smoking and drinking; they also serve as points of romantic encounter. In *Everybody Dies but Me*, staircases and landings figure as spaces of retreat for Katya when she runs away from home. In *Girls*, the most significant conversation among the three central protagonists in the film takes place on a staircase. In one respect, this reflects the reality of communal life in apartment blocks all over Russia: for years, landings and staircases were claimed by teenagers. There is also, however, a symbolic meaning in the representation of these spaces. The vertical axes of staircases provide conditions for placing the protagonist at different levels, sometimes precariously balancing, sometimes risking her or his life for a dare. These spatial arrangements allow Germanika to film characters using high and low angles, engendering a sense of anxiety and uncertainty. Moreover, staircases represent a liminal space between inside and outside, a potential means of escape, and a transitional device. Indeed, by placing her characters on staircases Germanika also places them in transit, opening up their stifling environment and providing a glimpse of escape.

The spatial arrangements of a doorstep, an entrance, a staircase, or a hallway also correspond to the Bakhtinian "chronotope" of threshold. The threshold is a space/action chronotope: it organizes the architectonic conditions in such a way that "crisis and break in life" can unfold. As Bakhtin notes, the chronotope of threshold thus has a highly metaphorical meaning; it is "connected with the breaking point of a life, the moment of crisis, the decision that changes a life (or the indecisiveness that fails to change a life, the fear to step over the threshold)."[22] The symbolic and metaphorical meaning of the threshold unites *Everybody Dies but Me* and *School*. Both texts position Germanika's protagonists on the edge; they have to deal with the possibility of crisis and break in life and they do so in a multitude of ways.

Staging the Becoming-Girl Movement

Germanika's teen protagonists cannot properly be described as a lost generation, however confused they may be. Against the stagnant background of the anemic Soviet landscape and oppressive school system they emerge as a force imbued with vital energy and dynamism. In this context it is even more striking that they conform to the description of teen experience—as Adrian Martin puts it, "that intense, suspended moment between yesterday and tomorrow, between childhood and adulthood, between being a nobody and a somebody, when everything is in question and anything is possible."[23] Their world is in flux; nothing is given or taken for granted, and its complex ethical and moral coordinates are constantly being worked out. Alliances are formed and quickly broken, friendships emerge and disintegrate, love and commitment are constantly questioned, and the world of adults is repeatedly rejected because it does not provide answers.

While the morphing and mutation of teen identity and subjectivity are the subjects that most generally preoccupy Germanika, it is the girls at the center of *Everybody Dies but Me* whom I pose as exemplary. What emerges through these characters is a complex picture of young women in the process of "becoming-girl." According to Deleuze and Guattari in *A Thousand Plateaus*, the girl . . . is an abstract line, or a line of flight. Thus girls do not belong to an age, group, sex, order or kingdom: they slip in everywhere, between orders, acts, ages, sexes: they produce *n* molecular sexes in the line of flight in relation to the dualism machines they cross right through. . . . The girl is like the block of becoming that remains contemporaneous to each opposable term, man, woman, child, adult. It is not the girl who becomes woman; it is becoming-woman that produces the universal girl.[24]

Contemporary feminist scholars such as Claire Colebrook, Driscoll, and Rizzo have drawn on Deleuze's arguments concerning bodies, identities, and becoming to think about subjectivity and sexual difference in new ways. As Colebrook notes, the foregrounding of the girl as a figure of becoming in Deleuze holds promise in terms of subverting not the dichotomy of man and woman but the dichotomy of being and becoming. While man "is traditionally defined as being: as the self-evident ground of a politics of identity and recognition," the figure of the girl "is invoked as the becoming of becoming." Because the girl must become a woman, she offers the opening of becoming and thus provides a way of thinking of woman not in terms of complementarity to man but in terms of "instability that surrounds any being."[25]

The feminist appropriation of Deleuze's concept might prove to be the most promising way to think about Germanika's oeuvre. Germanika strives to mobilize her position between the worlds of past and present, documentary and fiction filmmaking, and independent and commercial cinema as the very condition of her creativity. Her creative work is not owned by identities but is directed toward difference. Germanika's endeavor can be theorized as part of a feminist project, if feminism is understood not as one movement among others but, as Driscoll suggests, as a new way of thinking of movements as becoming.

From this perspective, Germanika's young female protagonists represent the process of becoming not as a movement toward something tangible and definable—aims, ideals, or images of themselves—but as a movement forward. Not motivated by rejecting the past or by achieving a specific image of the future, the girls' primary raison d'être is to exceed the limits of what they already have. Their bodies, identities, and subjectivities are constantly becoming different from themselves. Their trajectories do not represent the becoming of some subject. Rather, they embody agency without goals, agency encompassed purely by change and transformation. Among Germanika's characters, Katya, Vika, and Zhanna of *Everybody Dies but Me* embody Deleuze and Guattari's becoming-girl image most clearly. In the case of each girl, it is her capacity to become different from herself that is so central to her transformation and mutation throughout the film. With regard to Deleuze's concept of difference, Rizzo notes: "The true difference here is that subjectivity is open to change and change is the condition of the subject."[26] Similarly, Germanika's film does not work toward the construction of a particular subjectivity but rather clears space and preserves an openness to various possibilities.

This openness to possibility is found in narrative and characterization; it also organizes mise-en-scène, determines cinematography, and controls editing. Narrative, characters, time, and space are interdependent. There is a corresponding openness to possibility in the method that Germanika employs in working with her actors. She is renowned for her confident and meticulous control of the filming process, which some critics have gone so far as to describe as authoritarian. At the same time, there is little rehearsal: Germanika rarely does multiple takes. She also rejects props and the use of doubles—her actors drink alcohol and draw blood, the dialogue is only provisionally scripted, and there is substantial room for improvisation. As a result, Germanika's actors are forced to act in particular circumstances instead of performing certain actions. Broadly, the director instigates events in front of the camera rather than staging performances, leading to heightened authenticity and blurring boundaries between documentary and fiction. This method contributes to the unfolding of the process of becoming for its participants and viewers through events that constitute such becoming as well as through movements and improvisations that disrupt it.

Germanika's method also corresponds to the peculiar temporality of her works: in Bakhtinian terms, the sense of an intensified present. This sense goes hand in hand with the seeming simultaneity of the real time of the viewing process and the fictive time of the characters. Both the construction of the text and an encounter with the text thus become an event in the Deleuzian sense. As Colebrook writes, "To become through writing is to create an event."[27]

The distinctive temporality and radical open-endedness of Germanika's works create the conditions for such an event to take place. The finale of *School* leaves the series's multiple narrative lines not only unresolved but far more complicated than they were at the beginning. The possibilities contained within the series's finale make it open toward the future. Similarly, *Everybody Dies but Me* ends abruptly with a shot of Katya leaving a conversation with her parents to escape into her room, where we last see her for a brief moment sitting on the floor next to the desk. The film's final shot is compellingly ambiguous, and it is this ambiguity, even more than the heroine's resourcefulness, that leaves viewers with a sense of hope rather than despair. It also makes *Everybody Dies but Me* a film not about the past, or even the present, but primarily about the future. John Berger notes that all films are "anticipatory" in the sense that they make the viewer wait for what is to come next.[28] *Everybody Dies but Me* is radically anticipatory, not only in terms of events that take place over the five days that the girls were expecting so eagerly, but also in terms of their undefined future, which is left beyond the film's narrative. This is a becoming into the future in a truly Deleuzian sense, staged as becoming toward difference rather than toward any pre-given sense of subjectivity. The film creates the palpable sense that this future is near at the same time as it leaves its contours undefined.

Conclusion

My analysis takes up contemporary feminist thinkers' suggestion that the encounter between Deleuze and feminism can be extraordinarily productive. The activation of singularity and becoming as opposed to the valorization of a particular identity can help to address the "woman question" in Russia. For a country with a tragic totalitarian history, the acknowledgment of the irreducible singularity of every human being has an added urgency. By staging the becoming-girl movement through her unresolved, anticipatory narratives and by foregrounding the protean singularity of her characters, Germanika opens a space to think about subjectivity in modern-day Russia in new, complex, and productive terms.

Notes

1. Vikki Turbine, "What Does the Pussy Riot Case Tell Us about the Status of Women's Human Rights in Russia?," e-International Relations, 27 May 2013, e-ir.info/2013/05/27/what-does-the-pussy-riot-case-tell-us-about-the-status-of-womens-human-rights-in-contemporary-russia.

2. In terms of production cost, Germanika's budget ranges from US$200,000 for her forthcoming feature *Yes and Yes* (*Da i da*) to US$12,000,000 for the TV serial *A Short Course on How to Live a Happy Life* (*Kratkiy kurs schaslivoy zhini*, Channel One Russia, 2012), while Nikonova made her debut *Twilight Portrait* with the extreme budget of US$20,000 using a still camera.

3. Lynne Attwood, *Red Women on the Silver Screen: Soviet Women and Cinema from the Beginning to the End of the Communist Era* (London: Pandora, 1993), 103.

4. Hilary Pilkington, "'Youth Culture' in Contemporary Russia: Gender, Consumption, and Identity," in *Gender, Generation, and Identity in Contemporary Russia*, ed. Hilary Pilkington (London: Routledge, 1996), 196.

5. Kevin M. F. Platt, "The Post-Soviet Is Over: On Reading the Ruins," *Republics of Letters* 1, no. 1 (1 May 2009), arcade.stanford.edu/rofl/post-soviet-over-reading-ruins.

6. Julia Lesage, "The Political Aesthetics of the Feminist Documentary Film," in *Issues in Feminist Film Criticism*, ed. Patricia Erens (Bloomington: Indiana University Press, 1990), 228.

7. Anikó Imre, "The Age of Transition: Angels and Blockers in Recent Eastern and Central European Films," in *Youth Culture in Global Cinema*, ed. Timothy Shary and Alexandra Seibel (Austin: University of Texas Press, 2007), 71, emphasis in original.

8. The significance of the three central heroines is confirmed by the film's working titles, "Three Girls" and "KVZ."

9. Catherine Driscoll, *Teen Film: A Critical Introduction* (Oxford: Berg, 2011), 66.

10. Andrei Aleshin, "School and Life," *Russian Newspaper*, 13 January 2010, rg.ru/2010/01/13/szkola.html; Maria Agranovich, "Class on the Big Screen," *Russian Newspaper*, 2 March 2010, rg.ru/2010/03/02/alenikov.html.

11. Jane Knox-Voina, "'Everything Will Be OK': A New Trend in Russian Film," *Russian Review* 56, no. 2 (1997): 286.

12. Andrei Shigolev, "'Everybody Dies but Me,' directed by Valeria Gai Germanika," *Kinoart*, February 2009, kinoart.ru/ru/archive/2009/02/n2-article9.

13. Aleksandr Kolbovskii, "Valeriia Gai-Germanika: *Everybody Dies but Me* (*Vse umrut, a ia ostanus*, 2008)," trans. Birgit Beumers, *Kinokultura*, October 2008, kinokultura.com/2008/22r-vseumrut.shtml.

14. Teresa Rizzo, *Deleuze and Film: A Feminist Introduction* (London: Continuum, 2012), 33.

15. See Germanika's website, germanika.kinoteatrdoc.ru.

16. Kolbovskii, "Valeriia Gai-Germanika: *Everybody Dies but Me*."

17. Lily Avrutin, "The Soldier, the Girl, and the Dragon: Battles of Meanings in Post-Soviet Cinematic Space," *Cinema Journal* 38, no. 2 (1999): 75.

18. Jon Lewis, *The Road to Romance and Ruin: Teen Films and Youth Culture* (New York: Routledge, 1992), 3.

19. On narrative complexity in relation to television long form, see Jason Mittell, "Narrative Complexity in Contemporary American Television," *Velvet Light Trap*, no. 58 (2006): 29–40.

20. Hubert J. M. Hermans and Harry J. G. Kempen, *The Dialogical Self: Meaning as Movement* (San Diego: Academic Press, 1993), 46.

21. See Zygmunt Bauman, *Liquid Life* (Cambridge: Polity, 2005).

22. Mikhail Bakhtin, "Forms of Time and of the Chronotope in the Novel," in *The Dialogic Imagination: Four Essays*, ed. Michael Holquist, trans. Caryl Emerson and Michael Holquist (Austin: University of Texas Press, 1981), 248.

23. Adrian Martin, *Phantasms* (Melbourne: McPhee Gribble, 1994), 68.

24. Gilles Deleuze and Félix Guattari, *A Thousand Plateaus: Capitalism and Schizophrenia*, trans. Brian Massumi (Minneapolis: University of Minnesota Press, 1987), 276–77.

25. Claire Colebrook, introduction to *Deleuze and Feminist Theory*, ed. Ian Buchanan and Claire Colebrook (Edinburgh: Edinburgh University Press, 2000).

26. Rizzo, *Deleuze and Film*, 62.

27. Colebrook, introduction to *Deleuze and Feminist Theory*, 6.

28. John Berger, "Stories," in John Berger and Jean Mohr, *Another Way of Telling* (London: Writers' and Readers' Publishing Cooperative Society, 1982), 279.

Julia Vassilieva teaches film and television studies at Monash University. Her research interests include historical film theory and criticism, classic and contemporary Russian cinema, and Russian art criticism and cultural studies. She has published in the *International Journal of the Humanities*, *Senses of Cinema*, *Rouge*, *Continuum*, *Screening the Past*, *Film-Philosophy*, and *Kinovedcheskie Zapiski*. She is a coeditor, with Constantine Verevis, of "After Taste: Cultural Value and the Moving Image," a special issue of *Continuum* (2010).

Figure 2. *Everybody Dies but Me*

Figure 1. Darlene Johnson, writer and director,
Crocodile Dreaming (Australia, 2006)

Between Worlds: Indigenous Identity and Difference in the Films of Darlene Johnson

Therese Davis

Australian Indigenous writer and director Darlene Johnson's biographical documentary *River of No Return* (Australia, 2008) tells the story of Frances Djulibing Daingangan, a Yolngu woman from a small and extremely remote Indigenous community in Arnhem Land in Northern Australia.[1] At age forty-five, Daingangan was selected by Rolf de Heer to play the lead female role of Nowalingu in his arthouse hit *Ten Canoes* (Australia, 2006), codirected by Peter Djigirr and made in collaboration with the Indigenous community in Ramingining. Johnson's film documents Daingangan's life as she attempts to continue to pursue an acting career. It opens with a dreamlike image of the swirling motion of a spinning dancer: a young Yolngu girl in a pink party dress scored by the distinctive sound of Marilyn Monroe's singing "I Wanna Be Loved by You" from Billy Wilder's classic Hollywood farce *Some Like It Hot* (US, 1959). As the dance slows and the girl's features become clearer, Daingangan begins her voice-over narration: "As a child I always wanted to become an actress, just like Marilyn Monroe. But I was told it was ridiculous for a Yolngu girl to have such dreams, such fantasies." A close-up of the girl looking bewildered dissolves to a medium shot of Daingangan as she appeared in her role as Nowalingu in *Ten Canoes*, with her naked breasts decorated with the distinctive white clay markings of traditional Yolngu ceremonies. Here, however, Daingangan is not playing the role of an ancient Yolngu ancestor as she did in *Ten Canoes*. Rather, by affectionately emulating her movie idol in a soft, unaccompanied delivery of Monroe's signature song, she proves that far from being "ridiculous," her childhood dream of being an actress who can play any role she chooses has indeed come true.

This opening sequence from *River of No Return* cleverly dramatizes a long history of female film spectatorship through its figuration of Daingangan as a child caught in the reveries of wish fulfillment. As the story unfolds, the film becomes a testament to the ways in which the cinema can change the course of people's lives. It is also a vivid example of how Indigenous filmmakers are using film in highly inventive ways to expose the enormous social gap between Aboriginal communities—especially those located in rural and remote areas—and the wider Australian community. By bringing contemporary Indigenous culture and Hollywood cinema together in this intimate scene of mimetic performance, Johnson's film opens the way for a woman-centered perspective on the complexity of Australian Indigenous film as it emerges from the intersecting histories of colonialism and the cinema and the interplay of local and global cultures.

As Faye D. Ginsburg, Lila Abu-Lughod, and Brian Larkin have observed, studies of Indigenous media have been "'haunted' by the question of whether minority or dominated subjects can assimilate media to their own cultural and political concerns or are inevitably compromised by its presence."[2] As Australia's most prominent Indigenous documentary maker, Johnson is part of a group that Ginsburg describes as "a young Aboriginal cultural elite engaged in constituting a vital Aboriginal modernity through a variety of media, including music, visual arts, film, and drama."³ Most recently, this work has included a wave of feature films that present a new set of questions about the status of Indigenous media in the Australian imagination.

The films in this new "Blak Wave" have been widely celebrated and critically lauded: *Samson and Delilah* (dir. Warwick Thornton, Australia, 2009) received the Caméra d'Or at Cannes, *Bran Nue Dae* (dir. Rachel Perkins, Australia, 2009) won the People's Choice Award at the Toronto International Film Festival, *Toomelah* (dir. Ivan Sen, Australia, 2011) was honored with the UNESCO Award at the Asia Pacific Screen Awards, and *The Sapphires* (dir. Wayne Blair, Australia, 2012) swept the Australian Academy of Cinema and Television Awards.⁴ *The Sapphires*, a feel-good musical about an Aboriginal girl group from the 1960s, took in AU$2.3 million in its opening weekend and went on to become only the fifth Australian film in the past five years to gross more than AU$10 million at the local box office.⁵ The Weinstein Company rolled it out globally, and it spent several weekends among the top twenty films in the US.⁶ The commercial success of this and several other recent Indigenous features overturns the local industry myth that "stories with indigenous themes were box-office poison."⁷ It is also transforming the status of Indigenous filmmaking in the industry. As Sandra Levy, chief executive of the Australian Film, Television, and Radio School, recently claimed, "Indigenous screen practitioners have become a force to be reckoned with. . . . [They] are now firmly at the heart of contemporary screen practice."⁸

Yet while there is much to celebrate about this new wave of Indigenous features, there are some concerns about the marketing and popular discussion that surrounds it, namely the claim that Indigenous film is novel. The dominant national funding body, Screen Australia (formally the Australian Film Commission), continuously searches for new ways to make Australian cinema distinctive and competitive in the international market. This approach has played and continues to play a major role in the formation of this cinema's recognizable cycles: the quirky comedies of the 1990s, the reconciliation cycle of the 2000s, and the post–*Wolf Creek* (dir. Greg McLean, Australia, 2005) horror film cycle, which marked a radical shift in screen policy toward genre films. The problem with seeing Indigenous filmmaking as something novel is that it reduces the social and political difference of Indigenous filmmaking to a taste category or, as director Rachel Perkins recently put it, "the Indigenous brand."[9]

According to television producer Miranda Dear, non-Indigenous audiences have been steadily building an "appetite" for this new so-called brand of Australian film. She says: "It's been a natural evolution up to this moment, where there are these filmmakers ready to tell these [Indigenous] stories on a very high level, with an audience ready and willing to watch . . . in fact growing more receptive and more hungry for [these stories]" (46). The problem with this teleological narrative of Indigenous filmmaking as "a natural evolution" from the margins to the mainstream is that it sidelines three decades of diverse forms of Indigenous documentary, short, and experimental filmmaking. Much of this output, including landmark features such as Tracey Moffatt's *Bedevil* (Australia, 1993) and Rachel Perkins's *Radiance* (Australia, 1998), has been produced by Indigenous women filmmakers. The narrative also suggests that Indigenous film is of significance mainly for what it offers non-Indigenous audiences, reinforcing an assimilationist attitude that it is always the dominant culture that absorbs and not the reverse—Indigenous cultures absorbing and transforming aspects of other cultures, including the cinema and its stars, for their own purposes (38). At stake here is an acknowledgment and understanding of the unique in-betweenness of Indigenous filmmaking as a specialist sector that operates within while remaining different from the Australian film industry through its address to both highly localized Indigenous audiences and mainstream culture.

In this article I will explore the difference of Australian Indigenous filmmaking through a closer look at the films of Darlene Johnson. Although Johnson is best known for her documentary work, she has also made several award-winning shorts. She was one of the first filmmakers to be funded by the Indigenous Branch of the Australian Film Commission (now known as the Indigenous Department of Screen Australia), a state-funded institution established in 1993 to identify and nurture Indigenous talent and to provide funding opportunities for Indigenous filmmakers, including directors of the new wave of features such as Perkins, Wayne Blair, Ivan Sen, and Warwick Thornton, to participate in the film and television industry. Johnson received similar state funding, and her career parallels the development of the Indigenous film sector itself. This sector has managed to operate simultaneously within the Australian industry and outside of it through distinctive practices of film development and funding, production methods based on Indigenous principles and protocols, and the telling of uniquely Indigenous stories and histories.

What interests me about this dual aspect of Johnson's work and makes it particularly significant at this critical turning point in the history of Indigenous filmmaking in Australia is that it offers us a valuable commentary on the relationship between Indigenous film and mainstream cinemas, including Australian national cinema and international entertainment cinemas. I will show that in counterpoint to the perception that Indigenous filmmaking has "sprung up overnight,"[10] Johnson's films reveal that Indigenous Australians have a long and complex history of involvement in the global system of cinema as performers, filmmakers, and spectators. As shorts and television documentaries, Johnson's films clearly mark the importance of decades of Indigenous activist and community-based media while showing in their style and subject matter the importance of cinema and television for Indigenous people as a transformative imaginary within society and a source of pleasure.

This article privileges historical and biographical accounts to foreground the locatedness and historicity of Australian Indigenous filmmaking. In particular I want to mark Johnson's place in postcolonial Australia as a young, urban Aboriginal woman who has spent her life not only moving between the Indigenous and non-Indigenous worlds but also working in a film industry where directing continues to be dominated by white men.[11] I argue that Johnson's work is particularly useful for showing the complexity of the in-betweenness of Indigenous people's experience of the postcolonial world in which they now live, whether they are located in the city or a remote community. My method also uses film as a conceptual model—the process of thinking film through film. Johnson has made a number of films, including several biographical documentaries of Indigenous film actors, that document and/or narrate subjects whom she describes as "caught between two worlds."[12] These films speak to the very specific historical conditions of living under official Australian state policies such as assimilation, forced removal of Indigenous children from their families, and, more recently, the Northern Territory National Emergency Response Intervention.[13] They allow us to see the ways in which Indigenous people have used and continue to use film and video as a means of actively resisting these policies—including the Australian government's screen policies and institutions—and negotiating differences. I argue that Johnson's films offer a model of Indigenous filmmaking as the inventive work of inhabiting two worlds at the same time, like the art of film acting that she is fascinated by and beautifully documents; thus, as Marcia Langton suggests, they remake Aboriginality "over and over again in a process of dialogue, of imagination, of representation and interpretation."[14]

Becoming a Filmmaker

Johnson's first film, *Two Bob Mermaid* (Australia, 1996), was one of six short dramas featured in the Indigenous Branch's inaugural anthology *From Sand to Celluloid*.[15] It is set in a small, rural Australian town in the summer of 1957. Based on the filmmaker's mother's experience as a lighter-skinned Aboriginal girl growing up in the postwar assimilationist period, it tells the story of Koorine's (Carrie Prosser) dream of becoming a swimming champion. She discovers that she can get around a law from that time banning Aboriginal people from public swimming pools by passing as a white person. At the pool she meets a group of girls who shares her passion for swimming and invites her to join their team at an upcoming swimming carnival. But when the girls reveal their racist attitudes, Koorine chooses her family and culture over the pursuit of her dream.

Two Bob Mermaid was acclaimed for its treatment of the complex issue of racial passing from a child's point of view, and it continues to be used in Australian classrooms as a resource in antiracist education.[16] Less attention has been given to the prominence it gives to popular entertainment as a space of Indigenous pleasure and fantasy. There is, for example, a stunningly beautiful underwater shot in a scene at the swimming pool where Koorine and her white friends mimic the water ballet routines of Koorine's idol Esther Williams in *Million Dollar Mermaid* (dir. Mervyn LeRoy, US, 1952), a popular biopic of Australian swimming legend Annette Kellerman. Koorine's desire to be "just like Esther Williams," as she says, is an example of cross-cultural identification in film, something that *Two Bob Mermaid* itself addresses. In a scene at her home on the fringe of a small rural town, we see Koorine rehearsing the Esther Williams ballet routines against a backdrop of white bedsheets her mother is hanging from the washing line. The beleaguered mother barely notices her daughter, let alone recognizes, as we do, the obvious pleasure Koorine finds in imitating Williams's dance routines. When Koorine confides to her mother that she wants to become "a million dollar mermaid, just like Esther Williams," her mother scoffs: "A 'two bob' mermaid is more like it. You ever see any Black swimming champions? Swimmin'—that's for whitefellas."[17]

While *Two Bob Mermaid* is, as I mentioned above, based on Johnson's mother's experience, the story is also in some ways analogous to Johnson's personal journey. In the early 1990s, when she was twenty years old and first set out to become a filmmaker, the profession in Australia was still something very much "for whitefellas." At the time, there were only a small number of Indigenous filmmakers and only two feature films by Indigenous directors, the best known being Moffatt's *Bedevil*. Just as Johnson's mother/Koorine was inspired by Williams, Johnson has stated that Moffatt was an inspirational role model for her.[18] There are some similarities between the two filmmakers. Like Moffatt, who was adopted into a white family, Johnson was separated from her mother at an early age. She is a member of Australia's Stolen Generations, having been forcibly removed from her mother under Aboriginal Protection laws that specifically targeted Aboriginal children of mixed heritage. As a ward of the state, Johnson spent a number of years in the care of an order of Catholic nuns. She was later "stolen" back by her mother and hidden from authorities. Johnson has described film as a source of both pleasure and comfort during her traumatic childhood. She recalls that when her mother was working as an office cleaner in the city she would be left on her own in Sydney's downtown cinema precinct to watch double features of Hollywood movies. Later, the nuns introduced her to television, and she claims that her favorite pastime was watching reruns of B horror films and other Hollywood genre films on television.

To date, all of Johnson's work falls within short-form categories: short dramas, one-hour documentaries, and made-for-TV documentaries for Indigenous programs such as *Message Stick* (ABC, Australia, 1999–2012). Belinda Smaill has called for greater recognition of these minor forms as an important site of women's filmmaking in Australia,[19] and as Adrian Martin has argued, these "minor" forms are often more transformative than features.[20] Like Moffatt's films, Johnson's are not straightforward social message films and many convey her love of genre film. But while Moffatt's experimental shorts, such as the internationally renowned *Night Cries: A Rural Tragedy* (Australia, 1989), have helped her to build an international career as a visual artist, Johnson has chosen to work closely with Indigenous communities, inventively transforming or, more specifically, Indigenizing everyday forms of screen practice and helping to make television a significant site of Indigenous intervention in Australia. This is not to say that her work is not seen outside of Australia. It circulates internationally as part of an emergent Indigenous cinema, and she has been successful in obtaining international funding. Her supernatural drama *Crocodile Dreaming* (Australia, 2006) was partly funded by a National Geographic All Roads Film Project seed grant, and she received development funding in 2012 from the International Sami Film Centre in Norway for a feature film set in Arnhem Land. Her work has also been exhibited at local and international women's film festivals, pointing toward the important forms of crossover between Indigenous cinema and women's cinema and the role of film in Indigenous women's postcolonial feminist strategies and visions.

Following *Two Bob Mermaid*, Johnson wrote and directed her award-winning documentary *Stolen Generations* (Australia, 2000), which was broadcast on prime-time television and came to play a significant role in the Australian history wars. In 1997 the federal government conducted an inquiry into policies of the forced removal of Aboriginal children of mixed heritage from their families throughout the twentieth century.[21] Its findings divided the nation around the question of a national apology, with the prime minister at the time refusing to offer one. Although *Stolen Generations* was not the first treatment of this issue by an Indigenous director (Moffatt's *Night Cries* also tackles the subject), it was a landmark film that brought actual voices of the Stolen Generations into the mainstream at a crucial time in this public debate. Its intimate style and the moving accounts of its three interviewees cut through the ongoing political discourse by generating affect. Most significantly, it served as a counterpoint to the dominant voices of neoconservative media commentators who were at the time questioning the validity of the testimony of the Stolen Generations.

National and international critical recognition of *Stolen Generations* helped to position Johnson as one of Australia's up-and-coming documentary filmmakers.[22] In 2001 she was commissioned by Hollywood-based Australian director Phillip Noyce to document the making of *Rabbit-Proof Fence* (Australia, 2002), an adventure-search film that dramatizes Doris Pilkington Garimara's account of her mother Molly Craig's extraordinary thousand-kilometer walk across the Australian desert in 1931 after escaping with two younger siblings from a state institution for "half-caste" Aboriginal girls.[23] *Rabbit-Proof Fence* has become an Australian classic and is to date the best-known account of the Stolen Generations. Its positive reception in 2002 was greatly aided by its cross-media marketing campaign, which included Johnson's making-of documentary *Following the Rabbit-Proof Fence* (Australia, 2002). The latter was broadcast in prime time on Australian commercial television prior to the film's release, and it was shown on high rotation by Australia's international airline Qantas throughout 2002.

As with most making-of documentaries, the impetus of *Following the Rabbit-Proof Fence* was to attract audiences, but it also works as a stand-alone production through its compelling story of the search for three young Aboriginal girls to play the main roles in *Rabbit-Proof Fence*. Building on an interest in film performance established in *Two Bob Mermaid*, Johnson's documentation of *Rabbit-Proof Fence*'s preproduction process and location shoots narrates the three girls' transformation from nonactors to star-quality performers. It emphasizes the girls' young ages (ranging from six to thirteen), tapping into film audiences' long-standing fascination with child performers. There is, for example, a memorable scene in which Noyce is holding auditions for the role of Daisy, the youngest girl, in a school hall. We are told that the young hopefuls have been cued to enter the room and try to convince Noyce that a child outside is missing. We watch as a number of young children perform this scene in the stagey mode of theatrical acting: amplified voices, surplus movement, and exaggerated gestures. They are all very cute, but we find ourselves joining with Noyce in the embarrassed laughter of spectators watching a badly acted film. Cut to the audition of Tianna Sansbury, the young actor who would go on to play Daisy. She transforms before our eyes from a performer to a fictional child through her startling ability to act in a way that appears as if she is not acting. Noyce later admits on camera that Sansbury's performance was so uncanny that he really did begin to wonder if a child outside was in danger!

Johnson's knack for capturing scenes such as this on camera demonstrates her deep interest in film's transformative power. In this instance her unmasking of the techniques of realist film acting shows that the believability of Sansbury's performance (evidenced in Noyce's suspension of disbelief) is not, as Stephen Heath theorizes in his discussion of the ways in which meaning is constructed in film through actors' bodies and voices, the effect of the actor disappearing into a role. Rather, it is the effect of figuration—an actor becoming a role and "making something which is absent and does not exist present."[24] Johnson's preoccupation with actors and the art of film plays a crucial role in the films she has made in Aboriginal communities in Arnhem Land. Not only do these films tell the stories of prominent Indigenous actors, they also allow us to see how Indigenous Australians from both urban and remote areas appropriate film to express new ways of being Indigenous. Indigeneity is shown as something that is vital and constantly in transformation through the ways in which these films highlight Indigenous actors inhabiting both Indigenous and non-Indigenous worlds and using traditional and modern forms of performance to transform both.

Making Films in Ramingining

Despite being, in her words, "an urban, fair-skinned Blackfella from Bondi Beach," Johnson has, to date, spent more time working in Arnhem Land, home to the Yolngu people, than anywhere else.[25] Arnhem Land's harsh terrain, tropical climate, and distance from areas of Australia that were colonized earlier, such as Sydney and Melbourne, have given it a special status in the Australian imaginary as "the epitome of isolation."[26] This is reflected in the many volumes of work by anthropologists on Yolngu culture and in its depiction in popular culture, perhaps most famously in *Crocodile Dundee* (dir. Peter Faiman, Australia, 1986). Johnson was first invited to visit Ramingining, a small Aboriginal settlement in northeastern Arnhem Land, by the legendary Australian actor David Gulpilil, known for his starring and supporting roles in international and Australian film classics such as *Crocodile Dundee*, *Walkabout* (dir. Nicolas Roeg, UK, 1971), *Storm Boy* (dir. Henri Safran, Australia, 1976), and *The Last Wave* (dir. Peter Weir, Australia, 1977) as well as many more recent films such as Baz Luhrmann's *Australia* (Australia/US/UK, 2008), *The Tracker* (dir. Rolf de Heer, Australia, 2002), and *Rabbit-Proof Fence*. Johnson and Gulpilil met on the set of *Rabbit-Proof Fence*. He was playing a key role as a Black tracker; Johnson, as we know, had been commissioned to direct the film's making-of documentary. Johnson says that Gulpilil, who had seen her documentary *Stolen Generations*, approached her with an invitation to make a documentary about his life.[27]

The two collaborated on *Gulpilil: One Red Blood* (Australia, 2002), which Johnson wrote and directed. The project was her first experience of making a film in and with a "tradition-oriented community"—a community where the majority of people continue to practice traditional Aboriginal cultural forms of everyday life, such as hunting, food preparation, and spiritual ceremonies, alongside modern ways of living. In an interview with me she explains how an understanding of Indigenous cultural protocols was crucial to the method of filmmaking she developed in this context, where cultural and gender differences played an important role. As she explains, these protocols began with Gulpilil's invitation. She says that she would never have considered the possibility of making a documentary about Gulpilil's life herself because it would not have been culturally appropriate for her as a then young Aboriginal woman to initiate that relationship. Once she arrived in Ramingining, Johnson also had to form relationships with Gulpilil's extended family or "mob" (a term commonly used by Aboriginal people to refer to both Aboriginal and non-Aboriginal forms of social organization such as a family or an institutional group): "To make a film there you have to have a *real* relationship with the mob, you have to become part of the mob." She describes the method of filmmaking she developed in this environment as "working from a cultural perspective." This entails Johnson developing practices that accord with cultural traditions based on an Aboriginal autochthonous worldview, in which humans belong to the land and have responsibilities to it as the originator of law and culture. For example, Johnson explains that when she is developing a film script with the community in Ramingining, primacy is given to the cultural connection of humans and land. In her words, "how I find the story or understand the [film's] purpose or its meaning—that cultural specific that I hope will resonate in the film—is to wait for it to come from the people that have a connection to that place.... You have to remain open to the culture, the spirituality of the people and the place and allow the story and characters to evolve and manifest." Time is a crucial factor in this process. Building relationships and trust with a community takes time, and more than ten years later Johnson is still building that trust as she returns to make films. As an Aboriginal filmmaker she sees her role as one not of documenting cultural knowledge (ethnography) but rather of helping to maintain Aboriginal culture as it is lived in a modern world. She sees filmmaking as "a responsibility": "To be given the job of looking after cultural knowledge [through filmmaking] is a huge privilege."[28]

At the same time that Johnson was being initiated into a tradition-oriented community through important protocols like being given a designated role within the traditional kinship system of this language group, she was also operating as a contemporary filmmaker by initiating members of the community into the social and technical processes of filmmaking. In Ramingining she came to recognize herself as a woman director: "There were interesting encounters with the mob because I'm a woman and it was kind of different for them to see a Blackfella—a *female* Blackfella—making films . . . I think it was good for them to see me, a Black woman, outside of a traditional female role. In fact my nickname was 'boss woman,' because they could see that I was directing and, you know, bossing my white male crew around [she laughs]—organising things and getting things done, taking the lead [role]."[29]

Johnson carried this work of blending traditional Aboriginal practices and modern ways of doing things into the conception of her film as a social biography of an actor "caught between two worlds":

I remember wondering why no one had made a documentary about [Gulpilil] before this. As we know, he is an iconic figure with an amazing acting career that spans over three decades. . . . I thought about how I could do justice to this person who has lived a really rich, complicated, and, at times, conflicted lifestyle; someone who still lives the traditional way and moves in between that and contemporary Australian life. I had to think about how I would go about approaching a project that was primarily a profile or a social biography of someone who has been misrepresented, someone who I saw as being caught between two worlds.[30]

The film presents a loosely chronological narrative of Gulpilil's life story. More important, it provides Gulpilil with the opportunity to reframe and revise the received image of him as an Aboriginal stereotype. For more than three decades, Gulpilil has been the face of Aboriginal Australia and the archetype of the authentic traditional man or "noble savage." But he has a keen sense of irony, and in *Gulpilil* we see how he undercuts this image both on and off the screen.

Eschewing contemporary taste for intimate, psychological biographies, the film interweaves observational scenes of Gulpilil's everyday life in his community, where traditional Aboriginal cultural practices of hunting and spirituality—such as his performance in a boy's initiation ceremony—are practiced alongside his work as a film actor. Johnson allows him to assert creative control by performing a number of roles: subject, storyteller, and actor. The film also employs direct address, reversing the cinematic history that has quite literally silenced Gulpilil. In films such as *Walkabout*, *Rabbit-Proof Fence*, and *Australia*, he speaks either very few words or none at all. The setups of the direct-to-camera speeches in *Gulpilil* vary wildly as the camera and Gulpilil position the spectator as a guest, explicitly inviting and guiding the spectator subjectively through the mix of modern and traditional practices that composes the day-to-day life of the contemporary Yolngu world. This world appears in contrast with the reified Yolngu culture depicted in countless ethnographic films made in the region, including ethnographic recordings of Gulpilil as a young man participating in ceremonies, which are reappropriated here as part of his personal story. Low camera angles situate the viewer on the ground, where Gulpilil is framed cross-legged as he tells anecdotes from his life. Mobile camerawork allows us to walk side by side with him across his traditional lands as he explains sites of spiritual significance. A wide shot of the interior of the one-room house where he lives with his large family shows him explaining directly to the camera that the dilapidated dwelling is typical of the houses provided by the government in this area. These framing techniques combine with the present tense of Gulpilil's first-person narration to create a dynamic self-performance that invites us into the here and now of contemporary Yolngu life.

This self-performance is intertwined with film clips from Gulpilil's oeuvre; archival footage of him on the red carpet at Cannes and other international film festivals; documentation of him on location; and interviews with well-known directors (Noyce, de Heer), other actors (Justine Saunders, Jack Thompson), and Indigenous scholars (Gary Foley, Langton). Interviewees testify to Gulpilil's extraordinary talent as an actor and the cultural significance of his work. By switching back and forth between worlds and between Gulpilil's roles within these worlds, the film radically shifts the frame through which the spectator sees and can come to understand Indigenous culture and everyday life. At the same time, the film does not shy away from difficult aspects of Gulpilil's life in his community. Viewers learn that he has experienced forms of loss and exclusion within the Yolngu world as a consequence of his career as an actor. These costs include separation from his family, addiction to drugs and alcohol, jail sentences for crime related to addiction, and punishment for breaking traditional laws resulting in periods of exile. The film does not idealize life in the tradition-oriented community, nor does Gulpilil express any regret about his career as an actor. In a medium shot of him standing on his traditional lands near Ramingining, Gulpilil speaks directly to the camera, expressing his desire to be recognized as both actor and Yolngu:

I did a lot for the people [of Ramingining]. I did a lot for Australia and the outside world. Why? Because I've got a language and culture. One Red Blood. Who am I that God made me and left me here on the earth? Well I am here to share my culture and language. And this is where I live [pointing around him]—a poor part of the country, Arnhem Land. . . . We are the brothers and sisters of the world. Doesn't matter if you're bird, fish, snake, or kangaroo. One Red Blood.

This statement is a conscious demand for long-overdue recognition by the Australian film industry and audiences. It is also a demand for recognition of an Aboriginal worldview in which everything is connected: humans, animals, and the land. As Romaine Moreton notes, Johnson's film provides Gulpilil with the first opportunity "to speak directly to the world as himself, rather than through the [stereotyped] characters through which he has become known locally and internationally."[31] It also allows him to demonstrate his artistry as an actor and how he has used it to negotiate differences between Aboriginal worlds and the wider Western world as well as differences that occur within Aboriginal worlds.

This Is Not *Ten Canoes*

In 2005 Johnson returned to Ramingining to make *Crocodile Dreaming*, a film based on Gulpilil's mother's Dreaming story—a particular mode of story integral to Aboriginal spirituality that is given to a child by her mother and that determines the child's relationship to a particular part of the country, certain animals, and other people.[32] In the interim Gulpilil had initiated a collaboration with Australian director de Heer to make a feature film. This resulted in the much-celebrated arthouse film *Ten Canoes*, a project that has been the subject of numerous scholarly articles. De Heer himself has written a memoir about the production in which he addresses Gulpilil's reportedly conflicted relationship with his community and a falling-out between Gulpilil and others that led Gulpilil to abandon *Ten Canoes* in midproduction.[33] Interestingly, in interviews Gulpilil makes a point of differentiating *Crocodile Dreaming* from other film projects he has been involved in, including *Ten Canoes*. He says, "*Crocodile Dreaming* is my mother's Dreaming. It's not *Crocodile Dundee*; it's not *Ten Canoes*. . . . It's my true story." What Gulpilil means by "my true story," however, is anything but straightforward.

Crocodile Dreaming is set in the present. This makes it strikingly different from other films of Dreaming stories, including *Ten Canoes*, which typically represent the Dream Time as a mythical world. This representation reproduces the prevalent misconception that Aboriginal belief or the Dreaming posits "a finished universe fashioned by creation powers who retired into inaction once the age of primary genesis was done."[34] Johnson states that "it was important to [Gulpilil] that we represented Yolngu spirituality in a modern, contemporary world." She says that he also specified that the film should appeal to the younger generation in Ramingining. This represented a unique opportunity for her as a filmmaker: "I was given permission by [Gulpilil] to create a fictional story inspired by the crocodile Dreaming legend, to bring my own artistic and directorial vision to the creative process. It's important that people understand that it's not the real crocodile Dreaming legend. It's not an adaptation. When I pitched the scenario to David he was all for it, and his only desire was to make it entertaining. And I thought, 'Yeah, I can do that!' "[35]

The film's hybrid style reflects Gulpilil and Johnson's collaborative approach. On the one hand, its story about two estranged half brothers meets Gulpilil's aim of promoting Aboriginal spiritual beliefs and practices to Yolngu youth. Gulpilil plays the role of the elder brother Burrimilla, a Yolngu actor based in the city who is shooting an advertisement directed by Johnson (playing herself in a cameo role). Burrimilla is forced to return home to his traditional lands when his estranged, lighter-skinned brother Charlie (Tom E. Lewis) meddles with a sacred object, upsetting the balance of the spiritual world and thus creating havoc in the physical world. The two brothers come together in a quest to restore harmony to the world by returning the sacred object to its rightful place. Their journey includes a scene in which Gulpilil performs a spectacular mimetic ritual from the actual crocodile Dreaming ceremony in which he and others draw on the powers of the crocodile to become crocodile.

But the film is also inflected with Johnson's sensibility and speaks to her personal story. Her style involves adopting the adventure-search narrative and using special effects typically found in the horror/slasher and supernatural genres—the film styles she loved as a child. As a story about a man who has been alienated from his Aboriginal community and its traditional law and culture returning to his mother's country, the film is shot through with conflicted feelings of loss and longing that express the experience of the Stolen Generations and an emotional intensity typical of Hollywood melodramas. In the final scene, set on a majestic rocky outcrop in their mother's country, Burrimilla urges Charlie to call out to their mother's spirit to help him to remember the Dreaming story once given to him in this sacred place. The significance of this return to country and culture is emphasized through Johnson's choice to cast Tom E. Lewis in the role of the younger, lighter-skinned Charlie. Lewis is known in Australia for his outstanding performance as Jimmie Blacksmith in Fred Schepisi's *The Chant of Jimmie Blacksmith* (Australia, 1978), a dramatic account of the infamous historical case of a young, exploited Aboriginal man who explodes with rage and kills his white wife and others. In 2005, Indigenous director Ivan Sen made an international award-winning documentary, *Yellow Fella* (Australia), in which Lewis reflects on the way in which he has been haunted by that role as an unforgettably violent image. Lewis's performance as Charlie in *Crocodile Dreaming* works against that cinematic history through its image of reconciliation with cultural law and self-healing.

What I am suggesting is that the truth of *Crocodile Dreaming*—"my true story," as Gulpilil says—lies in the film's embodiment of the presentness of Indigenous culture and the hybridity of Aboriginal realities. As yet another example of Johnson's reflexivity and her focused attention to acting and the art of performance more broadly, *Crocodile Dreaming* points to the significance of imagination and art in the Indigenous worldview. Making this film was thus a deeply political act of performing Indigenous culture rather than simply representing it or trying to preserve it. By helping to restore the awe and mystery of storytelling—by maintaining the enchantment of the world—Johnson's filmmaking again refigures the space of contemporary Australia as a place where it is possible to be both Yolngu and modern at the same time.

Hollywood Dreaming

After completing *Crocodile Dreaming*, Johnson embarked on *River of No Return*, her third film project in Ramingining. The film grew directly out of the *Crocodile Dreaming* project, in which Daingangan played the role of the spirit mother. During the latter film's postproduction process, Johnson learned that Daingangan's childhood dream was to be a film actor. But not just any actor: Daingangan wanted to be, in her words, "an actress just like Marilyn Monroe," whom she had first seen in *The Seven Year Itch* (dir. Billy Wilder, US, 1955) in the 1960s at an outdoor cinema in the tiny Aboriginal settlement of Milingimbi in Arnhem Land. Johnson says: "I thought to myself that you cannot get any further removed from Aboriginal traditional culture than Marilyn

Monroe, and I wondered what it was about Marilyn that resonated with Frances."³⁶ From this starting point, Johnson teamed up with renowned documentary producer Patricia "Pat" Fiske to begin to document Daingangan's attempts to continue pursuing an acting career.

As with Johnson's other projects in Ramingining, *River of No Return* reflects the collaborative process of its making. The film is part observational documentary and part drama, with reenactments by Daingangan and her voice-over narration. Unlike the Aboriginal men's stories in *Gulpilil* and *Crocodile Dreaming*, told partly as a way of returning home and addressing Yolngu youth, Daingangan's story is directed at a wider audience. In other respects it is similar to *Gulpilil*, with Daingangan's voice-over guiding us through her world. She proudly introduces us to her grandchildren, her mother's river country, her elders, and her love of movies, the latter through a staged scene where she watches Marilyn Monroe in *Gentlemen Prefer Blondes* (dir. Howard Hawks, US, 1953) with her grandchildren. The female address of this story is clearly legible in its attention to aspects of Daingangan's life as a woman and the primary provider for her grandchildren: shopping for food in town, hunting and fishing for food on her traditional lands, teaching her grandchildren, grieving the loss of her mother, and overcoming the trauma of an abusive relationship. We learn in the course of the film that Daingangan lives independently and that she was the first woman in Ramingining to take out a domestic restraining order against her now former husband.

The film's title and script invite us to compare Daingangan's story to Otto Preminger's adventure-western *River of No Return* (US, 1954). Monroe plays Kay, a showgirl whose fiancé, gambler Harry Weston (Rory Calhoun), has abandoned her on a remote farm owned by widower Matt Calder (Robert Mitchum), who lives there with his son Mark (Tommy Rettig). Fearing an attack by "Indians," the trio begins a treacherous journey by raft down a river to the nearest settlement. Like Kay, Daingangan also finds herself abandoned. Following *Ten Canoes*, she is unable to return to her past life because, as she says, "Since travelling overseas [to the Cannes Film Festival] people started to change toward me . . . and tell me that I'm becoming too much like Balanda [white people]." Finding herself unable to fit back into life at home and not yet having arrived in the new life that she imagined her work in *Ten Canoes* would provide, Daingangan applies to study at an Indigenous performing arts college downriver in Brisbane. She tells us that she is compelled to undertake this journey because she wants to test her ability as an actor and thus, in her words, "prove who I am." Despite what others may think, Daingangan has come to know herself as an actor.

Her approach to self-transformation marks a significant difference between the narratives of the two *River of No Return* films. Unlike Kay, Daingangan does not turn to men and marriage as means of escaping her position as a subject caught between worlds. Instead, like Monroe, she seeks recognition outside of marriage through acting.

In this regard, Johnson's film resonates most strongly not with its namesake but with Hollywood women's films of the 1930s and 1940s. In his reading of a group of these films, which he calls "the melodrama of the unknown woman," Stanley Cavell argues that the position of women in relation to conflicting worlds is different from that of men: "The position of woman is neither that of exiles nor of immigrants: unlike the immigrant, the woman's problem is not one of not belonging but one of belonging, only on the wrong terms; unlike the exile, the woman is not between two different cultures but is at odds with the one in which she was born and is roughly in the process of transfiguring into one that does not exist, one as it were still in confinement."[37] This double dilemma of a woman being at odds at home and seeking a new world into which to arrive—"one that does not exist"—aptly describes the conflicts of Daingangan's situation as an "unknown woman," that is, as an Indigenous woman seeking to be recognized as modern in a postcolonial society where she has been consigned to the role of a so-called authentic, traditional Aboriginal.

For Cavell, the unknown woman's search for the right to tell her story takes the form of a creative act of metamorphosis, "some radical, astonishing, one may say melodramatic change of the woman, say of her identity" (6). He suggests that this alternative route is represented most clearly by those female movie stars of classical Hollywood cinema who represent what he describes as "glamorous independence": Greta Garbo, Marlene Dietrich, Bette Davis, Barbara Stanwyck, and Ingrid Bergman (7). In this vein, Johnson's *River of No Return* documents the "astonishing" and indeed "melodramatic change" of Daingangan's identity in and through her professional identification as a film actor and having had a film made about her as an actor. Archival footage of Daingangan at the world premiere of *Ten Canoes* at Cannes shows her on the red carpet twirling for the cameras in a glamorous evening dress not unlike the famous white halter-neck dress Monroe wore in *Seven Year Itch*. This image of Daingangan itself swirls as it is dissolved with others in a montage of scenes from her performance in *Ten Canoes*. We watch Daingangan watching herself on the big screen being recognized for her talent as an actor.

Yet *River of No Return* also documents the limitations of this Hollywood dream for Daingangan. For while film can provide women with a potential alternative path to integrity and recognition—a life of "glamorous independence"—Johnson's film shows that this kind of freedom does not apply evenly to all, reminding us of the continued dominance of whiteness in English-language cinemas. The film ends with Daingangan receiving the news that her application to the performing arts school has been rejected. This result suggests that there is yet no place for Daingangan to arrive where she can act other than as she has been inscribed, that is, as a traditional Yolngu woman. Daingangan is limited by her Indigenous difference as it is currently understood. In this way, the film reveals underlying racial politics that preclude the possibility in contemporary Australia of an Aboriginal woman's desire to be "like Marilyn Monroe." Desiring to be "like" Monroe does not, I suggest, mean that Daingangan wants to imitate a normative and outmoded white femininity, as Monroe's star image has come to represent.[38] Rather, it expresses a desire to be free to act differently, the necessary freedom of any artistic performance.

In defiance of these limitations, however, the film performs a happy ending for this story. Despite rejection, Daingangan, like many of the great female characters of the classic women's melodramas, triumphs in the face of defeat. For while the performing arts school may not have recognized her talents, her collaboration with Johnson on this project ensures that she is projected in and through *River of No Return* as larger than life. In the final moments of the film we see Daingangan in the twilight, walking along the red dirt road that winds its way through the tropical wetlands and maze of rivers of her traditional lands, speaking to Noyce on her mobile phone. We hear Noyce encouraging her to pursue her dream of becoming a professional actor. Furthermore, her performance in this scene—and indeed throughout the film—is recognized by us, the audience she and Johnson have gathered through this inventively directed performance of self that has been broadcast on television and shown at international film festivals. As one film critic put it, *River of No Return* is "a film that makes us weep with frustration at the obstacles Frances faces, and laugh with glee at her sense of humour and tenacity."[39] In other words, the film allows us to recognize that Daingangan shares many of the qualities she admires in her idol Monroe: great comedic timing, "a sweet voice," and the astonishing, some say magical, ability to transform herself through film acting and thus potentially to change the way audiences see the world.

Conclusion: Mermaids, Movie Stars, and Film Directors

The mermaid figure has a special significance in both Johnson's work and her personal story. In the 1950s Johnson's mother performed as "Obelia the Million Dollar Mermaid" in the sideshow alleys of agricultural shows across Australia. This "high-class" aquarium act, as one newspaper reported, was performed in a large glass tank and involved novelties such as her mother eating bananas under water.[40] According to Johnson, her mother's work as an entertainer allowed her to live a fairly independent life. This was remarkable in a period when women's social mobility in general was restricted by the norms of a patriarchal society that confined them to domesticity, and when most Aboriginal people were segregated from society, living on special reserves with their mobility controlled by various state Aboriginal Protection acts that required them to report their whereabouts to the state.[41] Johnson's mother's independence from state control was possible only because she was not publicly identified as Aboriginal. An advertisement from that time promotes her as "Obelia, the Million Dollar Mermaid who is from Florida, USA."[42] *Two Bob Mermaid* invokes this true story, manifesting a chain of trans-Pacific mimetic exchange between Indigenous cultures and Hollywood throughout the twentieth century: Johnson's mother passing as white and imitating the US "million-dollar mermaid" Esther Williams who, in the musical biopic *Million Dollar Mermaid*, acted as Australian swimming champion Annette Kellerman, who in her heyday as a star of the silent screen passed herself off in *Venus of the South Seas* (dir. James R. Sullivan, US/New Zealand, 1924) as a Polynesian princess![43] So when Johnson was asked by All Roads to produce a profile of herself as a filmmaker to help promote a video compilation that includes *Crocodile Dreaming*, it is not so surprising that she chose to include an underwater scene of herself swimming naked, mermaid-like.[44] Here, Johnson doubles as her mother while also putting herself on display for the big screen, like female movie stars she admired as a child. But this is not a performance of passing or a masquerade. Rather, in her nakedness she becomes a mythical creature, shedding the outer skins of racial identity imposed on her and other Indigenous women. Like the underwater shots from *Two Bob Mermaid*, this is a fluid image of unbounded movement in which she performs the freedom of unknownness as the power to endlessly alter one's identity. This arresting image can also be taken as a powerful figuration of her role as an Indigenous woman director who helps to keep Indigenous filmmaking vital and transformative in and through her ability to move fluidly between worlds.

Notes

The broader framework of this essay is informed by my collaborative research partnership with multitalented Indigenous filmmaker and philosopher Dr. Romaine Moreton on a project funded by Screen Australia titled "Remapping the Remote/Urban Divide in Australian Indigenous Film," and a new project with Chris Healy on international aspects of Indigenous cultural production. The analysis of Johnson's work is entirely my own. I especially want to thank Darlene Johnson for making time to discuss her work with me and for trusting me with her personal story. I would also like to thank Belinda Smaill, Patricia White, Jodi Brooks, and Lalitha Gopalan for the very helpful feedback I received from them on early drafts.

1. Which term to use when referring to the original inhabitants of Australia has been a fraught political question. This essay follows the recommendation of the Australian government's *Style Manual*, 6th ed. (Milton, QLD, Australia: Wiley, 2002), to use *Aboriginal* (with a capital *A*) as a noun to replace *Aborigine*. *Indigenous* is the preferred inclusive adjective to encompass both Aboriginal and Torres Strait Islander peoples. I use a capital *I* for "Indigenous" when referring to Indigenous Australian peoples and cultures and lowercase *i* when referring generically to indigenous peoples around the world. Many Indigenous Australians prefer to be known by the tribal group to which they belong. Yolngu is the name that Aboriginal people in Arnhem Land use to refer to themselves.

2. Faye D. Ginsburg, Lila Abu-Lughod, and Brian Larkin, introduction to *Media Worlds: Anthropology on New Terrain*, ed. Faye D. Ginsburg, Lila Abu-Lughod, and Brian Larkin (Berkeley: University of California Press, 2002), 9.

3. Faye D. Ginsburg, "Screen Memories: Signifying the Traditional in Indigenous Media," in Ginsburg, Abu-Lughod, and Larkin, *Media Worlds*, 49–50.

4. For educational background information on the "Blak Wave," see the Australian Centre for the Moving Image permanent exhibition in Melbourne or "Blak Wave 2010," www.acmi.net.au/global/docs/Blak_Wave_Education_Resources.pdf (accessed July 2013).

5. Brendan Swift, "*The Sapphires* Passes *Tomorrow When the War Began* on All-Time Box Office List," *Inside Film*, 4 October 2012, if.com.au/2012/10/04/article/The-Sapphires-passes-Tomorrow-When-the-War-Began-on-all-time-box-office-list/CBGXDVQJKN.html.

6. Neala Johnson, "*The Sapphires* among the Top 20 Movies at the US Box Office," News.com.au, 16 April 2013, www.news.com.au/entertainment/movies/the-sapphires-among-the-top-20-movies-at-the-us-box-office/story-e6frfmvr-1226621705601.

7. Jim Schembri, "15 Landmark Indigenous Films," 3AW 693 News Talk, 15 August 2012, www.3aw.com.au/blogs/denis-walter-blog/15-landmark-indigenous-films/20120815-24887.html.

8. Sandra Levy, "Cinema Culture Richer after Rise of Indigenous Voices," *Sydney Morning Herald*, 5 June 2013, www.smh.com.au/comment/cinema-culture-richer-after-rise-of-indigenous-voices-20130604-2no4e.html.

9. Quoted in Ed Gibbs, "The Rise and Rise of Indigenous Stories on Screen," *Lumina: Australian Journal of Screen Arts and Business*, no. 11 (2013): 38.

10. Erica Glyn, head of the Indigenous Department of Screen Australia, counters this point of view in Andrew Urban, "Indigenous New Wave," *Urban Cinefile*, 9 June 2011, www.urbancinefile.com.au/home/view.asp?a=17870&s=Features.

11. From 1971 to 2011 the overall proportion of men and women working in the Australian film and television industry has remained steady, with women composing around 35 percent of the workforce. See "Number and Proportion of Male and Female Producers, Directors and Writers of Australian Feature Films, 1970–2011," www.screenaustralia.gov.au/research/statistics/oefilmmakersff.aspx (accessed July 2013). In 2008 the Australian Film Commission tracked women writer, producer, and director participation in the one hundred Australian feature films released between 2003 and 2007. It found that women wrote sixteen, directed thirteen, and produced twenty-three of these features. See www.wift.org/about/Marian%20Evans%20Notes%20May%202008.pdf. There were no feature films directed by an Indigenous Australian in this period. Since 2009, ten feature films have been directed by Indigenous Australians, including three by women.

12. "Darlene Johnson on Making Films in Arnhem Land: An Interview," by Therese Davis, *Screening the Past*, no. 31 (2011), www.screeningthepast.com/2011/08/darlene-johnson-on-making-films-in-arnhem-land. Johnson has two feature projects in development as writer and director: "Baru," a transnational project set in Ramingining and being made with the assistance of the International Sami Film Centre, Norway, and "Obelia," a film based on her mother's life that is currently at script development stage and being produced by Phillip Noyce.

13. For more information on the intervention, see *The Intervention: Katherine, NT* (dir. Julie Nimmo, Australia, 2008), and *Our Generation* (dir. Sinem Saban and Damien Curtis, Australia, 2010).

14. Marcia Langton, *"Well, I Heard It on the Radio and I Saw It on the Television": An Essay for the Australian Film Commission on the Politics and Aesthetics of Filmmaking by and about Aboriginal People and Things* (Sydney: Australian Film Commission, 1993), 33.

15. *From Sand to Celluloid*, directed by Richard Frankland et al. (Lindfield, NSW, Australia: Indigenous Branch of the Australian Film Commission, 1996), DVD.

16. *Two Bob Mermaid* received national and international recognition; it was an official selection at the Venice International Film Festival's "Window on Images" in 1996 and won Best Short Dramatic Film at the Forty-First Asia-Pacific Film Festival and Best Short Film at the 1996 Australian Film Critics Circle Awards.

17. "Two bob" is an Australian and UK colloquialism for two shillings (twenty cents). It is commonly used to denote insignificance. "Whitefella" (from "fellow") is an Aboriginal colloquialism for a non-Aboriginal person of European descent. It applies to both men and women. *Macquarie Dictionary*, s.vv. "two bob," "whitefella," www.macquariedictionary.com.au (accessed July 2013).

18. See Sista Girl Productions, "Darlene Johnson on a Politics of Filmmaking," Australian Centre for the Moving Image, 2009, generator.acmi.net.au/gallery/media/politics-filmmaking. See also Darlene Johnson, "Aboriginality and the Politics of Representation," *Photofile* (Australian Centre for Photography), no. 40 (1993): 32–35.

19. Belinda Smaill, "Cinema against the Age: Feminism and Contemporary Documentary," *Screening the Past*, no. 34 (2012), www.screeningthepast.com/2012/08/cinema-against-the-age-feminism-and-contemporary-documentary/.

20. Adrian Martin, "Whispering in Our Hearts," *Rouge*, no. 6 (2003), www.rouge.com.au/6/whispering.html.

21. Human Rights and Equal Opportunity Commission, *Bringing Them Home: Report of the National Inquiry into the Separation of Aboriginal and Torres Strait Islander Children from Their Families*, 1997, www.humanrights.gov.au/sites/default/files/content/pdf/social_justice/bringing_them_home_report.pdf.

22. *Stolen Generations* received several international awards, including the Grand Jury Journalist Award for Best Documentary (Prix du Jury AFJ) at the 2001 Festival International de Films de Femmes in Paris and the prestigious Golden Gate Award in the History category at the 2001 San Francisco International Film Festival.

23. Doris Pilkington Garimara, *Follow the Rabbit-Proof Fence* (Brisbane: University of Queensland Press, 2002).

24. Stephen Heath, "Body, Voice," in *Questions of Cinema* (London: Macmillan, 1979), 179–82, as quoted in Paul McDonald, "Film Acting," in *The Oxford Guide to Film Studies*, ed. John Hill and Pamela Church Gibson (Oxford: Oxford University Press, 1998), 32.

25. "Darlene Johnson on Making Films in Arnhem Land."

26. Regina Ganter, "Myth at the Brink of History," in *The Art of Politics/The Politics of Art*, ed. Fiona Foley (Southport, QLD, Australia: Keeaira, 2006), 10–17.

27. "Darlene Johnson on Making Films in Arnhem Land."

28. "Darlene Johnson on Making Films in Arnhem Land," emphasis in original.

29. "Darlene Johnson on Making Films in Arnhem Land."

30. "Darlene Johnson on Making Films in Arnhem Land."

31. Romaine Moreton, "Curator's Notes: *Gulpilil: One Red Blood*," *Australian Screen*, aso.gov.au/titles/documentaries/gulpilil-one-red-blood/notes/ (accessed July 2013).

32. For a more detailed explanation of the role of Dreaming stories in contemporary life, see Basil Sansom, "Irruptions of the Dreamings in Post-Colonial Australia," *Oceania* 72, no. 1 (2001): 1–32.

33. Rolf de Heer, "A Toxic Mix," *Griffith Review*, no. 16 (2011), griffithreview.com/edition-16-unintended-consequences/a-toxic-mix. It should be noted that Gulpilil returned to the project in postproduction to perform the film's distinctive narration, which was written by de Heer. For more discussion of this project, see Therese Davis, "'Remembering Our Ancestors': Cross-Cultural Collaboration and the Mediation of Aboriginal Culture and History in *Ten Canoes*," *Studies in Australasian Cinema* 1 (2007): 5–14.

34. Sansom, "Irruptions of the Dreamings," 2.

35. "Darlene Johnson on Making Films in Arnhem Land."

36. "Darlene Johnson on Making Films in Arnhem Land."

37. Stanley Cavell, *Contesting Tears: The Hollywood Melodrama of the Unknown Woman* (Chicago: University of Chicago Press, 1996), 23.

38. See Richard Dyer, "White," *Screen* 29, no. 4 (1988): 44–65.

39. Irina Dunn, quoted in "*River of No Return*," Ronin Films, www.roninfilms.com.au/feature/1526/river-of-no-return.html (accessed 23 July 2013).

40. "Obelia: The Million Dollar Mermaid," *Northern Miner*, 27 June 1953, 2.

41. "Darlene Johnson on Making Films in Arnhem Land."

42. Advertisement, *Cairns Post*, 21 July 1953, 9.

43. Angela Woollacott, "Annette Kellerman: Mermaids and South Sea Islanders," in *Race and the Modern Exotic: Three Australian Women on Global Display* (Clayton, VIC, Australia: Monash University Publishing, 2011), 39.

44. *All Roads Film Festival: Fifth Anniversary Collection*, directed by Katja Gauriloff et al. (Washington, DC: National Geographic Society, 2008), DVD.

Therese Davis is the author of *The Face on the Screen: Death, Recognition, and Spectatorship* (Intellect, 2004) and coauthor, with Felicity Collins, of *Australian Cinema after Mabo* (Cambridge University Press, 2004). She has published articles on Australian Indigenous film and television in *Studies in Australasian Cinema, Screening the Past, Continuum, Senses of Cinema,* and *Interventions.* She is head of film and television studies at Monash University.

Figure 2. Frances Djulibing Daingangan. *River of No Return* (dir. Darlene Johnson, Australia, 2008)

Figure 1. Mia Wasikowska, Lisa Cholodenko, and Julianne Moore on the set of *The Kids Are All Right* (dir. Lisa Cholodenko, US, 2010)

The Kids Are All Right, the Pursuits of Happiness, and the Spaces Between

Jodi Brooks

One of the most surprising aspects of Lisa Cholodenko's 2010 film *The Kids Are All Right* (US) is the amount of publicity and discussion that it both received and generated.[1] The film seemed to be carried into cinemas atop a wave of media attention and much collective back patting at the proclaimed liberalism of US screens. *The Kids Are All Right* was discussed on talk shows and entertainment shows, in women's magazines and interior design publications, in broadsheets and tabloids, and in various lesbian, gay, and queer publications and forums. Even if a lot of the talk was about how much the film was being talked about, *The Kids Are All Right* was still talked about a lot.

Films by American female directors working in the indie sector—the film had a budget of around $4 million—rarely get this much publicity or comment, even when they have prominent or respected Hollywood actors in lead roles. Focus Features, distributor of *The Kids Are All Right*, launched the film with a sizeable marketing campaign that helped to move the film into cinemas

Camera Obscura 85, Volume 29, Number 1
DOI 10.1215/02705346-2408534   © 2014 by *Camera Obscura*
Published by Duke University Press

and move audiences to the film. The film went on to win Golden Globe awards for Best Motion Picture and Best Actress and was nominated for four Academy Awards, including Best Picture. *The Kids Are All Right* was celebrated as marking a new moment in US popular cinema, a moment in which white, middle-aged, lesbian characters could carry a commercially successful film with broad audience appeal on the big screen at least once, and in which lesbian partners could both represent and occupy the trials and tribulations of long-term monogamous couples with children.

Playing to, and playing on, some of the hot points of contemporary US sexual politics—same-sex marriage, queer parenting, and transformations in reproduction and family formation—the film seemed to rehearse and model same-sex marriage and the queer family for a wide viewership. It did so by packaging them in the form of what we might call a model family—two parents (complete with a mostly stay-at-home mom), two children, and domestic labor confined to an offscreen space (and most likely to an offscreen staff). Yet the film's relation to that model family, in both its heteronormative and homonormative forms, has been a point of unease and dispute in the circulation and reception of the film.

The Kids Are All Right is Cholodenko's most commercial and commercially successful film to date and the most divisive in its reception. While it has been celebrated by liberals, the film has also been taken to task and denounced for its homonormativity. Indifference to this film is not, it seems, an option.[2] Much of the debate around the film, particularly in online queer forums, has concerned how appealing its depiction of same-sex marriage and queer parenting is or should be to the film's audiences. For some, the film is an important contribution to the marriage equality movement, either because of its warts-and-all portrait of a lesbian marriage or because of its rose-tinted portrait of a lesbian couple. For others, like Jack Halberstam in a particularly sharp critique of the film on the blog *Bully Bloggers*, the film does not even know what it is doing. Halberstam writes: "While the film's moral outcome is supposed to favor the women and leave Paul out in the cold, it actually delivers, *whether the film means to or not*, a scathing critique of gay marriage."[3]

Considering that *The Kids Are All Right* is a film in which particular and cherished American institutions—the middle-class family unit, the American dream—are inhabited by a couple of lesbians and their kids conceived with an anonymous sperm donor, and a film in which homonormative and homonationalist discourses around family are expressed through and occupied by lesbian characters, it is hardly surprising that the film's reception has been highly polarized. One of the things that makes the film both intriguing and troubling is precisely how it depicts these various occupations of institutions, discourses, and worlds and how it highlights what is lost and gained in inhabiting and moving between them.

Cholodenko's films have received little scholarly attention to date. This can partly be explained by the fact that she has only directed three theatrical feature films spread out over a twelve-year period.[4] In this respect, we might say that Cholodenko's cinema is a kind of "slow cinema" in which slowness is tied not to aesthetics or style but to lack of opportunity, which is the predicament of many female independent filmmakers.[5] Cholodenko's previous two feature films—*High Art* (US, 1998) and *Laurel Canyon* (US, 2002)—both premiered at Cannes and were critically acclaimed on the festival circuit. *High Art* won the Waldo Salt Screenwriting Award at the Sundance Film Festival, and Ally Sheedy won the National Society of Film Critics Award for Best Actress for her performance in the film. *High Art* is recognized as an important film in the development of new queer cinema.[6] But neither film caused much of a ripple outside the arthouse and queer cinema worlds. Cholodenko's films are often relegated to the footnotes in scholarly work on US independent cinema, as is the work of a number of other female American independent filmmakers.[7]

For all the media attention that *The Kids Are All Right* received, very little of substance was said about the film's relationship to Cholodenko's previous work.[8] As I will argue, there are similarities and continuities between the film and Cholodenko's earlier work that are worth attending to. Each of Cholodenko's films is about the spaces between different social, sexual, and subcultural worlds, and if a project, or at least theme, can be assigned to her work, perhaps it is about what it is to live and move—and to choose—between worlds. Like Cholodenko's previous two films, *The Kids Are All Right* is a film about crossing between worlds and the spaces between them. It highlights the spaces between queer and straight, between marriage and not-quite marriage, and between the imagined and the lived. And the film itself occupies an in-between space in cinema: between lesbian cinema and mainstream cinema, between advocacy film and comedy-drama, and even between film and television.

Attending to the various kinds of crossovers that the film's themes engage with and the crossover that the film undertakes in its perceived intervention into US film culture provides a way of understanding its polarized reception. More important, these considerations can highlight an aspect of the film that has gone largely without comment: the ways in which the film, and Cholodenko's oeuvre more generally, draws our attention to the spaces between worlds—to that which is lost, dismissed, or left to long for.

To understand how *The Kids Are All Right* charts these in-between spaces and itself occupies an in-between space as a result of its movements between different genres, audiences, and agendas, I will look at the film's textual aspects—including its color palette, juxtaposition of different rhythms of movement, and juxtaposition of scenes with music and scenes without—and read this film through and against Cholodenko's earlier work. First, however, I look at how the film's reception and marketing have been marked by and have often floundered over locating the in-between spaces that the film both depicts and occupies. To do so I return to the film's release and the intervention it was seen as making in US cinema and debates around same-sex marriage.

The Kids Are All Right as Crossover Film: Recognizability, Unrecognizability, and Ambivalence

The Kids Are All Right was pitched as a timely film—a film both of and for the times—and, in much of the publicity material for and opinion pieces about it, as a film that would show viewers how to get with the times. The story revolves around a family confronting the costs and benefits of controlling its boundaries and dealing with the desires and imagined futures that have been lost along the way. The central couple, Jules (Julianne Moore) and Nic (Annette Bening), have been together for much of their adult lives, and their interactions slip and slide between weary irritation, performed affection, and, less often, camaraderie. Their two teenage children—daughter Joni (Mia Wasikowska), who is on the cusp of departing for college, and son Laser (Josh Hutcherson), who is making his way through teenage masculinity—are the primary avenues through which the family's outside and inside worlds are brought into contact, most dramatically when the two children bring their sperm-donor father, Paul (Mark Ruffalo), into the mix. Marketed as a "dramedy" about Paul's impact on the family unit—"Nic and Jules had the perfect family until they met the man who made it all possible" was the extraordinary promotional tag line used on the film's poster and in its trailer—the film has been applauded, in affluent Anglophone cultures at least, as a film about American middle-class family life that "shows it like it is." The film's marketing campaign and ensuing discussions have framed the film through a bumper-sticker-style politics: whether hetero or homo, "marriage is hard" (as Jules states in her excruciating apology to her partner and kids), and embarrassing your children is part and parcel of being a parent.

The film was quickly taken up as a discussion piece in the same-sex marriage debate and in discussions around queer/rainbow families and same-sex parenting. The *Hollywood Reporter* described it as "a love letter to gay-marriage supporters," the *Village Voice* directly tied the film to same-sex marriage legislation, and GLAAD published a resource guide for the film on its website aimed at journalists and educators.[9] This discourse has not been limited to the US, where the film has circulated as an issue-based, feel-good film that can educate a broad audience. In Australia, the *Sydney Morning Herald* ran a promotional shot from the film's poster below the headline "Two Mums Better than One?" for an article that clearly drew on GLAAD's resource page. After a brief synopsis of the film, the article turned to a widely publicized study from the US journal *Pediatrics* about children who grew up in families with two lesbian mothers. It then transitioned to portraits of three Sydney lesbian couples with children.[10] In this way, it presumed a seamless connection between the cinematic and the real, a connection that has, unsurprisingly, been the source of much of the dispute around the film.

Both the marketing of *The Kids Are All Right* and the film itself have highlighted and played on the simultaneous recognizability and unrecognizability of its story for an imagined everyman or everywoman. As mainstream observers have mentioned repeatedly, it is the familiarity of the film's domestic world that makes it so appealing for some. In a story about the trials and tribulations of long-term monogamous relationships, recognizability and unrecognizability are also narrative themes: the long-term relationship at the center of the film feeds on and falters over the pleasures and disappointments of domestic familiarity and familiar domesticity. The familiarity of the domestic squabbles and small parenting blunders; the sharp put-downs given and received by both partners and teenage children; the remnants of desires and erotic pulls lost beneath a sea of daily routines, affections, irritations, and disappointments; the daily comforts and tedium of the upper-middle-class domestic environment that the family unit occupies—these are what the film offers through, and indeed places on, its lesbian parent couple.

The recognizability and unrecognizability of *The Kids Are All Right*'s domestic and cinematic terrain are central to the film's status as a crossover text. Discussing Stephen Frears's 1985 film *My Beautiful Laundrette* (UK), Kobena Mercer describes the crossover film as one in which "material with apparently marginal subject matter becomes a commercial success in the marketplace."[11] As a lesbian-themed film from a filmmaker readily associated with US queer cinema, marketed and played to a mainstream or at least broad audience, *The Kids Are All Right* meets some of our most familiar understandings of this category. It has also been likened to another recent crossover film that received significant media and critical attention, Ang Lee's 2005 film *Brokeback Mountain* (US), and has been hailed as a "lesbian Brokeback."[12] Much of the discussion that has taken place around *The Kids Are All Right* has focused on the costs or payoffs of the film's crossover status. Yet it is by no means the first crossover film to generate highly polarized responses across its different audiences, nor is it the first one to be addressed primarily in terms of its representational politics. Responses to the film have largely played out on familiar turf for films with lesbian, gay, and/or queer characters or themes, with much of the discussion focusing either on the moral compass of its characters and plot or on the moralism of the film itself. On the website AfterEllen, for instance, managing editor Trish Bendix wrote in her feature article on the film: "I'm not aiming to rehash the argument about whether Lisa Cholodenko was right or wrong to create a storyline in which Jules, a woman in a lesbian relationship, cheats on her partner by sleeping with a man. (*I think it's fair to say that cheating is wrong, in general. We can probably all agree on that.*)"[13] Given that much of the praise and criticism that the film has received has revolved around the sexual politics of the film's genre crossing, it is worth addressing the ways in which ideas of crossing over are not only central to the film's perceived intervention into US popular cinema and popular culture but also threaded through the film's story line and themes.

With the film's lesbian parents and their kids inhabiting both the cherished two-parent family unit in its white, suburban form and the American dream with its upwardly mobile generations, crossing over takes center stage in *The Kids Are All Right*. Crossing over is part of its narrative about aging, as the couple confronts middle-aged coupledom and their soon-to-be status as lesbian empty nesters. The crossing over of chromosomes from the anonymous sperm donor is also a theme, most clearly expressed in Jules's interest in recognizing the expressions and gestures of the children in donor Paul. Finally, *The Kids Are All Right* can be understood as involved in a crossover between different screen media: soon after the film's release it was reported that HBO was planning to develop a television series from the film, bringing the "two-mom" family unit into something close to regular programming on American screens—though whether the proposed series will actually go ahead seems to be still in question.

The film muses on the losses and gains of inhabiting privileged social institutions and cultural forms. While a conservative moralism courses through the film and seems to rise victorious at its close, the film also thwarts the possibility of any easy victory for homonormativity, leaving the casualties—desires and individuals—of constructing and maintaining the family all too audible at its borders. *The Kids Are All Right* is engaged in a push-and-pull with itself, in which attaining a look (homonormative, two-parent family; mainstream film) is marked by the very stasis that the film pulls against.

"I Wish You Could Have Been Better": Cinematic and Queer Disappointments

In her eloquent discussion of *The Kids Are All Right*—a discussion that appears, somewhat unexpectedly, in an essay on landscape—Jill H. Casid describes the film as an "exercise in cinematic wish un-fulfillment." Far from being a snide dismissal of Cholodenko's film, Casid's characterization instead homes in on the sense of discomfort that the film generates. *The Kids Are All Right*, Casid writes,

> dramatize[s] an experiment in not just the conjugal (a lesbian couple with two kids from a sperm donor) but also the inhabitation of a domestic version of the (very classed, very Anglo) American dream in the future perfect form (there, in the house and garden with the white picket fence, two parents, two kids, and a dog, will have been Paradise). While the unfinished garden (laden with sex, class, race, and gender stereotypes) at the center of the film points by negation off the frame to the promise of a landscaped utopia and dreams that never actually materialize, the film leaves its viewer instead with the aesthetics (and arguably the realities) of discomfiting humor and profound awkwardness: an exercise in cinematic wish un-fulfillment that rends a tear putting us closer to the real we don't want. When the lesbian couple's daughter rebuffs the sperm-donor-would-be-Dad with the words, "I thought you'd be, I don't know, better," we also hear the film's *mise-en-abyme*, its commentary on its own refusal to deliver the vital alternatives we may wish to see enacted and its insistence instead on exploring the difficult topography of disappointment and desire at that

place where the elastic rubber of the future perfect hits the rough road of reality-testing.[14]

Casid is not the first critic to suggest that *The Kids Are All Right* is not that forthcoming when it comes to wish fulfillment. But whereas much of the criticism of the film has been aimed at the characters' values, their world, and the apparent or assumed moralizing of the film, Casid draws attention to the place of disappointment in it.[15] Why is it that the forms of disappointment that course through the film and are a significant part of its story have received so little comment? To what extent might this be because these disappointments have been regarded as small losses? Even the most passing consideration of the film's casting would suggest that disappointment might be one of its themes. Julianne Moore has an impressive history of playing disappointed women in the domestic sphere—most notably, Cathy Whitaker in Todd Haynes's 2002 film *Far from Heaven* (US) and Laura Brown in Stephen Daldry's film of the same year, *The Hours* (US/UK)[16]—as does Annette Bening, with her role as the sparkly, efficient, and on-edge Carolyn in Sam Mendes's 1999 film *American Beauty* (US). How do the disappointments in *The Kids Are All Right*, and the film's ambiguous treatment of them, relate to and intersect with some viewers' disappointments with the film?

Casid identifies what might be one of the film's most unique features: not that it has two lesbian moms and their teenage kids living in a sunny, always blue-skied, suburban Venice Beach; not that it introduces the sperm-donor father who then has sex with one of the women, in the comedic move of having a biological father and biological mother have sex for the first time years after the child is born, and the woman, a lesbian, having to slap the sex out of him; and not even that it was a box office success. Rather, *The Kids Are All Right*'s uniqueness lies in how it makes poignant its refusal to provide the desired (cinematic) world that many viewers, and certainly many queer viewers, long for: one in which difference, or the recognition of difference, is possible—if not here and now, then someplace or sometime.

Mapping Worlds and the Spaces between Them: The Textual Work of Cholodenko's Films

The world of *The Kids Are All Right* is portrayed as considerably less seductive than the worlds of either of Cholodenko's previous films. While each of her films aims an almost surgical eye both at the pleasures and possibilities and at the dead ends and self-indulgences of their worlds, the sensory pleasures of the two earlier films are largely absent in this most recent one. Cholodenko's first two films revolve around worlds that are sexually knowing and visually and sonically intoxicating—worlds that turn around female characters who are charismatically indifferent to social expectations. *High Art* centers on the heady, half-charged world of its New York lesbian junkie art scene, with its ambience of stoned knowingness and endlessly raised, endlessly deferred sexual pleasure, all delivered through the temporal filter of the heroin dissolve. *High Art* crafts and unfolds this world through a camera that can never settle; bodies that become liquid as they slide from one position to another; and a sound track that, through the constant presence of reverb, seems steeped in the same sultry temporal waywardness as the image track.[17] *Laurel Canyon*'s world is the laid-back, swaggering cool of its LA music scene. With the film's story unfolding in the dream home of its titular setting—recording studio at one end, airy Richard Neutra house at the other, and steamy pool and overgrown garden in the center—the world of the film is the "fecund" garden imagined but never completed in *The Kids Are All Right*. In contrast to the sensuous spaces in these two films, the world in *The Kids Are All Right* is the suburban California home of the white, upper-middle-class family. Squarely framed with its interiors straight from an upmarket furniture catalog, the space of the family home is offered to view with the same frontality as the family home in *The Brady Bunch* (ABC, 1969–74).[18]

Each of Cholodenko's three feature films constructs a world through close attention to rhythms, color palettes, soundscapes, economies of movement, and temporal sensibilities. And in each of these films, the worlds that unfold attract others from outside their field. In *High Art*, this outsider is Syd (Radha Mitchell), ingenue and driven assistant editor of a photography magazine; in *Laurel*

Canyon, it is Alex (Kate Beckinsale); and in *The Kids Are All Right*, it is Paul. But *The Kids Are All Right* works somewhat differently from the previous two films. Its difference is not simply a matter of the apparent flip that makes the lesbian couple more similar to the straight characters in the first two films. Instead, its difference lies in its angle of vision on what it is to occupy privileged social and cinematic worlds.

In Cholodenko's previous two films, the charismatic characters occupy worlds with fluid boundaries: people, sounds, desires, and liquids are constantly spilling in and out of them. In *High Art*, friends are always coming into or out of the half-lit interior of Lucy (Ally Sheedy) and her girlfriend Greta's (Patricia Clarkson) apartment, lingering indefinitely in the shared slow time of their drug use. And while the water that seeps between Lucy and Greta's apartment and Syd and her boyfriend's apartment below brings the two spaces together and draws Syd into the world upstairs, just where that water has come from is never clear. "No one here has taken a bath recently," Lucy tells Syd, and indeed the only time the bathtub is used is to resuscitate Greta when she has overdosed. It is as if seepage itself—the aqueous movement between and across spaces—defines the film's world. Likewise, in *Laurel Canyon*, the music from the studio drifts up to the house where Alex is doing the final work on her dissertation and draws her down into the (also) half-lit world of the recording studio. Similarly, Jane's AC/DC T-shirt moves from Jane (Frances McDormand) to her current lover, Ian (Alessandro Nivola), and then to Alex, marking the movement of desires, openings, and connections. In many ways home, for Jane, is something with no clearly defined physical or proprietary borders: she has both the house in the canyon and another house, unseen, at the beach, which, she tells her son, Sam (Christian Bale), she has given to her most recent ex—much to Sam's indignation. Homes, assets, lovers—they are all always in constant movement for Jane. In contrast, in *The Kids Are All Right*, boundaries are secure and to be secured, and it is the threat to those boundaries—Paul's arrival and Joni's imminent departure for college—that drives the drama.

In *The Kids Are All Right*, Cholodenko depicts control over these borders, and the rhythms of the world that is contained within them, with the same precision with which she characterizes the movements between worlds in her earlier films. Those that threaten this world's borders are banished, and the film presents the expulsion of these figures with sharp frontal framing. When Paul is rejected by the family unit and comes to the family home to speak to Joni, we see him from the family's point of view, framed by the lounge room window as he tries unsuccessfully to be allowed in. When Luis (Joaquín Garrido), the Hispanic gardener employed to do the labor required to produce the "fecund" garden, is dismissed on the spot by Jules when she suspects he is aware of her sexual escapades with Paul, he is shot straight-on in center frame. The film both plays to an uncomfortable comedy and displays the collateral damage of the (homo)normative family unit and the forms of exclusion it practices and with which it collaborates.

The world of *The Kids Are All Right* bypasses the sensory headiness of both *High Art* and *Laurel Canyon*. Perhaps part of its disappointment lies in the fact that Cholodenko seems to have shirked her duty to make sexy films. All erotic force has been sucked out of *The Kids Are All Right*: life in the affluent 'burbs is filled with the forced smiles of irritated partners and sexual pleasures deferred by work phone calls and not being able to find the remote control. *High Art* has been praised for its "uncompromising" view of lesbian life in the midst of an ongoing call for "idealized images."[19] To what extent is *The Kids Are All Right* also an uncompromising view—albeit one that is less appealing, less sexy, more embarrassing, and more disheartening?

In one scene in *High Art*, Lucy and Greta's friend Arnie's (Bill Sage) birthday is celebrated by the apartment's full-time and part-time occupants along with Syd, who is spending more and more time hovering around them. Lucy, Greta, and entourage gather around a table in the foreground of the shot to wish Arnie a happy birthday; the candles are blown out; and the characters return to the depths of both the shot and the room, sinking back into the assortment of low-lying lounge chairs dispersed around the drug table. The cake is left untouched, of no interest to anyone—though Syd, remaining in the foreground of the shots, hovers around it for a moment longer before realizing that the rest of the group, indifferent to cake eating, has moved away. Compare this to the after-work marital kiss scene that occurs early in *The Kids Are All Right*, in which the viewer is first introduced to the family unit. Nic returns from work and joins the rest of the family at the dinner table in a medium shot that then cuts to a close-up as she comes in to deliver the obligatory peck to Jules. While the first scene carries humor that is hard to locate in the second, both are attentive to the bodily and spatial habits of their inhabitants through meticulous framing and timing. This is one example of how *The Kids Are All Right* shows the occupation of both social and cinematic space by bodies that are more readily placed outside these spaces' fields of vision. It is precisely this framing and foregrounding of the lesbian occupation of the model American family that sets *The Kids Are All Right* apart from Cholodenko's first two films.

The sensory sumptuousness of Cholodenko's earlier films is nowhere more notably absent than from the bedroom of *The Kids Are All Right*'s central couple. The color palette of the women's bed is satirically tasteful, even quietly abrasive: ivory headboard, lavender sheets, and dark champagne quilt—cold, reflective colors that sit together in uneasy, almost antagonistic, proximity. In scenes of the two women in bed, the dissonant colors fill the frame. It is only in scenes in which others, but not the couple itself, are in their room—as in the scene when Laser and his jock friend Clay (Eddie Hassell) hit the parental bedroom in search of contraband—that the film opens the room to a more harmonious color palette and reveals an outside (a balcony, perhaps?) that remains out of view in other shots of the room. Further, the dissonant, muted colors of the bedroom stand distinct from the colors used for other scenes in the house, particularly in the bedrooms of the two teenagers' rooms, and for other locations, including the garden under construction at Paul's Echo Park home, that home's interior, Paul's restaurant, and even the restaurant and bar where the two women erupt in argument in front of their straight-couple friends.

Lest viewers miss what is happening through the film's shifting color palettes, the film also orients us through its use of music. With original music composed by Carter Burwell, a title referencing a song (The Who's 1965 hit "The Kids Are Alright"), and a compilation score of music as diverse as David Bowie, Leon Russell, and Tame Impala, *The Kids Are All Right* gives considerable significance to its sound track. Unlike nearly every other scene in the film, the scenes with the couple are never set to music until the film's close: the music (nondiegetic or diegetic) stops as soon as we hit the door of the family home and enter the spaces of the couple/parents, leaving us to view them without any beat or movement other than that of their interactions or through the occasional fragment from Burwell's score, with its undercurrent of sonic distortion. The significant exception here is the scene in which Nic breaks into an awkward impromptu rendition of Joni Mitchell's song "All I Want." Claudia Gorbman describes scenes "when characters sing—not in the patently artificial artful song performances that we normally call musical numbers, but in moments that are construed and perceived as integral parts of the 'realistic' diegetic world"—as "artless singing."[20] But this scene, gently playing on the scene in *American Beauty* in which Bening's character also engages in some artless singing (she belts out Barbra Streisand's "Don't Rain on My Parade" as it plays on the car stereo before being stalled by the evidence of marital trouble before her), does not re-set the women to music. In *The Kids Are All Right*, Nic's artless singing—which occurs moments before she finds Jules's hair in Paul's bathroom sink—marks the distance between a then in which a future was imagined and a now in which another is lived.

The Kids Are All Right constantly juxtaposes scenes set to music with those that are not. The former are associated with freedom and cinematic wish fulfillment—such as when daughter Joni rides double on Paul's BMW motorcycle, the clichéd lesbian bike of choice, to the sound of Uh Huh Her's "Same High"—and the latter with stasis and responsibility. This dynamic is established in the film's opening scene as we follow Laser and Clay flying through suburban streets on cycle and skateboard, respectively. The camera weaves around them, seemingly caught up in the same momentum, and their movement is set to music. When we arrive at the family home, in a shot taken from the driver's seat of a moving car, this rush of movement is brought to an abrupt end. As we pull into the driveway in a shot common to countless US family dramas and sitcoms, the ignition is turned off, the music stops, and we enter the family home.

This music-terminating arrival plays to two readings at the same time: it carries a sense of loss, disappointment, and even horror for some viewers with the crossover into apparent homonormativity, while surprising others with the cinematic crossover of two lesbian mothers in an American comedy-drama. Through scenes such as this, the film's claimed timeliness is troubled by the movements and depictions of time in the film itself. On one hand, the strained tempo of the film, with its tension between a sense of stagnation and eruptions of movement, hampers any sense that the occupation of privileged social institutions (at a narrative level) and cinematic terrain (by the film itself) is without ambivalence. On the other hand, the present of the film's story, which has served as a kind of anchor for readings of the film as an advocacy text, is set adrift by the past and future losses that perforate that present.

Cholodenko creates film worlds with which we are never quite contemporary. They are like folds in the present, alternate worlds that track a different beat. With their tight plot duration and limited backstory, each of Cholodenko's films is like a suspended time capsule. Although set in a historical present shared with their audience, they occupy an else-when. *High Art*'s New York lesbian art scene is a world just past: Lucy is a former next-big-thing art photographer, her girlfriend Greta a former star of Rainer Werner Fassbinder's films. The film's sound places the whole story in something like a temporal loop: the reverb-heavy soundscape of the opening scene, in which Syd enters the subway, plays again in the scene midway through the film in which Syd and Lucy have sex, so it is never clear to which time in the plot this soundscape—associated with Syd's aural perspective—actually belongs. Comparably, *Laurel Canyon* takes place in a Laurel Canyon that lives in its own alternate time. In his book *Hotel California*, Barney Hoskyns quotes Cholodenko discussing her interest in the setting: " '[There's a] kind of irreverent, *Land of the Lost* thing that people get into up there in the middle of a high-pressure functioning city.' Cholodenko set her rock movie in Laurel Canyon because—despite the steady influx of lawyers and other professionals into the area—the place still seemed to her 'kind of lazy and kind of dirty and kind of earthy and sort of reckless.'"[21] Laurel Canyon here serves as a world that is both past and passing and yet strangely copresent, running on its own time—part of the film's historical present and, as is also the case in *High Art*, fracturing that present with pasts that remain. In *The Kids Are All Right* this fracturing of the present with failed futures of the past and feared futures of the present sits in tension with the film's claimed timeliness.

The Kids Are All Right also unfolds a parallel world embedded somewhere in the present, but the time of this world faces both ways. As Casid writes, the present of the film's story is shot through both by past hopes that have failed to materialize and by what I would call anticipatory grief. For Casid, the film explores "that place where the elastic rubber of the future perfect hits the rough road of reality-testing," but perhaps it is more the case that the future perfect—what will have been—is in constant tension here with what could have been. The film's claimed timeliness is in tension with its own temporal dislocation, tracking an empty present suspended between yesterday's dreams and tomorrow's losses and between yesterday's moribund institutions and tomorrow's dead ends and entrapments. (It is worth noting that in this film's what-will-have-been world, the lesbian couple is the only two-parent family that we see in the film.) It is here, in the film's movements between worlds and its tension between a what-will-have-been and a what-could-have-been, that *The Kids Are All Right* sends us somewhere else. Just what this space might be, both socially and cinematically, is, in the end, left in question.

As the film draws to a close and the credits begin to roll, the film hands itself over to its closing song, MGMT's 2009 "The Youth." Set in compound quadruple time of 12/8, this anthem-like song gives musical form to the film's own push-and-pull against itself. The four beats of its refrain ("The youth is starting to change / Are you starting to change / Are you / Together") sounds an almost drone-like dirge that keeps getting caught on the same two notes while the lyrical triplet notes above try to pull the song somewhere else, only and always to be pulled back again by the same repetitive four-beat structure. With its compound meter, "The Youth" is, perhaps, the perfect song with which to close the film, its unmelodic and repetitive four beats—as heavy and constrained as the institution of marriage and, perhaps, the limitations of the commercially successful crossover film—set against the rolling three beats that try to pull it, and viewers, somewhere else.

Locked Up in Homonormativity and Viewing Sideways: Leaving a Space for the Queer Viewer

For those wanting something like a lesbian-populated *The Awful Truth* (dir. Leo McCarey, US, 1937)—a queer comedy of remarriage that would blast apart marriage, transform festival into festivity, and release marriage from itself in favor of a broader spectrum of intimacies and forms of social connection[22]—*The Kids Are All Right* offers something more like the awful truth about homonormativity and the lesbian parent trap.[23] *The Kids Are All Right* raises the prospect that the awful truth might be that this is as good as it gets. Yet at the same time, the film's movement against itself, in its push-and-pull framing of the occupation of the model homonormative family unit, also sends viewers elsewhere—and certainly, by the end of the film, outside the home.

Figure 2. Nic (Annette Bening) and Jules (Julianne Moore) in *The Kids Are All Right*

One of the ways in which the film moves against itself and sends viewers elsewhere is through how it thematizes viewing practices that take their pleasures sideways. There are two key scenes in the film in which viewing sideways serves to articulate a kind of queer difference. Both show Nic and Jules watching something on television. The fact that the couple watches gay male porn in their bedroom has been much discussed, as has Jules's explanation to Laser of the detours that can be in play when lesbians are looking for good sex, or sex prompts, on-screen. In a scene that has received less attention, the two women watch the National Geographic Channel's exploitation television series *Locked Up Abroad* (UK, 2007–). Their choice of *Locked Up Abroad* as entertainment carries an ironic, if somewhat melancholic, humor. *Locked Up Abroad* is a series that reenacts the imprisonment of tourists while traveling, usually for attempting to smuggle something into or out of a country. *The Kids Are All Right* might also be seen as attempting to smuggle something into or out of American cinema and homes, though whether it has done so successfully remains a subject of dispute. And while Jules and Nic are pictured curled up on the sofa watching the Uganda episode of *Locked Up Abroad* in a rare moment of pleasure together, they are left watching it alone. Viewing sideways is, in the end, what the film's lesbian characters do.

Each of Cholodenko's films seems to sprout from the seed of a previous one. The idea for *Laurel Canyon*, Cholodenko has said, came from listening to Joni Mitchell's album *Ladies of the Canyon* (1970) when *High Art*'s editor, Amy Duddleston, had it playing in the cutting room. And Mitchell, in turn, was a slow throw to *The Kids Are All Right* eight years later, appearing both through the daughter's name and in Nic's artless singing. Across each of Cholodenko's films one signature shot recurs. This shot is the framing of a gesture in which a group of characters moves as one as they become aware of the presence of someone or something from outside the group. In *High Art*, it occurs when Syd, first noticing Lucy's photos across the lounge room wall, calls them to the attention of the cool but motley crew of regulars in Lucy and Greta's apartment. The group's heads loll back in unison to see the photographs behind them, momentarily drawn out of their drugged time by the newcomer. In *Laurel Canyon,* the same gesture occurs when the uptight son Sam enters the recording studio looking for his girlfriend, Alex. Lined up around the mixing desk, lightly stoned and leaning back in their chairs, the band members, Jane, and Alex turn in unison as they register his presence. In *The Kids Are All Right* the gesture appears a third time, in this case delivered by Jules and Nic as an invitation to Laser to join them for a hug as the couple watches *Locked Up Abroad.* Rejecting the offer, Laser replies, "Hug her; that's what she's there for," and heads out of the house. The appearance of Cholodenko's signature gesture here, in a scene of viewing sideways, seems to encapsulate the film's ambivalence about the homonormative space it depicts. In its scenes of viewing sideways the film acknowledges its own ambivalence over the ability of a crossover film to depict the spaces between worlds and what crossing between them entails, and gestures toward those spaces, releasing the viewer to the possibility of imagining something else.

The world that this film depicts has conjured an affectionate familiarity for some viewers while leaving others horrified. Clearly, different relations to the homonormative middle-class lifestyle of the lesbian characters and their offspring have played and continue to play a major role in whether the film is seen as an "uproariously funny," social-issue-based comedy-drama or something closer to a psychological horror film.[24] In many respects the polarized reception of the film has centered on the question of how the film portrays the lesbian occupation of the two-parent American family unit. Considering that the film was repeatedly described as "pitch-perfect," it is somewhat ironic that so much of the debate around the film has revolved around the issue of exactly which note the film is sounding.[25] This question is not simply an issue of the film sounding one note for one audience and a different note for another. While the film often plays with a form of dual address that is sometimes found in crossover films, what is more striking is how it manages to move between these two notes and, at times, hold them in tension. Burwell, the film's composer, offers a useful way of understanding the tone of the film and the tension between the different notes that the film has been seen as sounding. Commenting on the film's score, Burwell describes *The Kids Are*

All Right's "signature guitar sound"—a sound produced by using a "magnetic pickup on an acoustic guitar"—as "lend[ing] the score a mixture of warmth and distortion that seems quite appropriate to the story."[26] The word *distort* comes from the Latin *torquere*, "to twist"; *distort* includes in its meanings "to twist or wrench to one side," "to give an erroneous turn to," and "to alter to an unnatural shape by twisting."[27] Certainly there is much that one could see as being twisted or distorted in the film, though this will no doubt vary from one viewing position to another—ideas of marriage, queerness, family, and parenting are all set somewhat askew here. This idea of distortion, and of the interplay between distortion and warmth as central to the film's sound (and the sounding of its world), is another way of describing the film's push-and-pull against itself and the discordant note that it at times strikes.

As the time between the film's release and its viewing lengthens and the film no longer carries so heavily the burden common to many crossover films of making a timely intervention into contemporary cinema and representational politics, the film's own musings on what it is to cross over sexually, socially, and cinematically might sound more clearly and come into sharper view. If *The Kids Are All Right* can be seen as giving form to a world through attention to that world's rhythms and tonalities, then we might say that the note that it sounds is the discordant one of crossing over itself—tracing an ephemeral space that holds, precariously, the distance between different worlds.[28]

Notes

I would like to thank Therese Davis and Belinda Smaill for their comments and suggestions on an earlier draft of this essay, for inviting me first to speak about, and then to write about, *The Kids Are All Right*, and for their patience as I resisted doing both. I would also like to thank Viki Dun, Therese Davis, and Beck Maine for listening to many hours of my rambling thoughts on Cholodenko and comedies of remarriage, and Claire Perkins for her useful feedback on an earlier draft. Finally, I would especially like to thank Lynne Joyrich and Patricia White for their detailed and generous feedback on this essay.

1. While Cholodenko both wrote and directed her first two films, *The Kids Are All Right* was cowritten with Stuart Blumberg.

2. See, for instance, the following exchange between Margaret Pomeranz and David Stratton, the hosts of the ABC Australia television program *At the Movies*:

    > DAVID STRATTON: And as you say, it's interesting that almost nothing is made of the fact that they're a lesbian couple. They could easily be a heterosexual couple and have the same kind of problems—well, almost the same problems.
    >
    > MARGARET POMERANZ: I do think it adds an extra texture to the film, though.
    >
    > DS: It does, there's no doubt about that, but it's not stressed or overemphasized, it's just there. It's accepted. It's not—the kids don't find it particularly remarkable either, which is a nice touch, really. ("*The Kids Are All Right*," *At the Movies*, www.abc.net.au/atthemovies/txt/s2985212.htm [accessed 5 November 2012])

3. Jack Halberstam, "The Kids Aren't Alright!," *Bully Bloggers* (blog), 15 July 2010, bullybloggers.wordpress.com/2010/07/15/the-kids-arent-alright/, emphasis added. Halberstam continues:

    > If the message here is "see gay marriages are just like straight ones—we all face the same problems," then surely the outcome of the film would be the end of marriage, the desire to find other kinds of arrangements that work? But no, this film, like many a heterosexual drama that turns the family inside out only to return to it at the film's end, shows that marriage is sexless, families turn rotten with familiarity, lesbians over parent and then it asks us to invest hope into this very arrangement.

4. Cholodenko also directed the television movie *Cavedweller* (US/Canada, 2004), an HBO film based on Dorothy Allison's book of the same name, and, like many other directors working in the US independent film sector, she has directed a number of television episodes.

5. For a particularly insightful discussion of slow cinema and the recent debates around its merits, see Karl Schoonover, "Wastrels of Time: Slow Cinema's Laboring Body, the Political Spectator, and the Queer," *Framework* 53, no. 1 (2012): 65–78.

6. As B. Ruby Rich comments, *High Art* is a film that both "challenged people's expectations [in the queer film festival circuit] and crossed over into the arthouse circuit" and "upset utopian views of gay and lesbian relations as inherently more equitable or superior to their heterosexual counterparts." B. Ruby Rich, "Collision, Catastrophe, Celebration: The Relationship between Gay and Lesbian Film Festivals and Their Publics," in "Queer Publicity: A Dossier on Lesbian and Gay Film Festivals," special issue, *GLQ* 5, no. 1 (1999): 83, reprinted in B. Ruby Rich, *New Queer Cinema: The Director's Cut* (Durham, NC: Duke University Press, 2013).

7. While Cholodenko's work rarely receives attention in studies of contemporary US independent cinema, some recent books that have mentioned her work at least in passing include Chris Holmlund and Justin Wyatt, eds., *Contemporary American Independent Film: From the Margins to the Mainstream* (New York: Routledge, 2005); and Wheeler Winston Dixon, *The Second Century of Cinema: The Past and Future of the Moving Image* (Albany: SUNY Press, 2000). On *The Kids Are All Right*, see Karen Hollinger, *Feminist Film Studies* (New York: Routledge, 2013). On *High Art*, see Lee Wallace, *Lesbianism, Cinema, Space: The Sexual Life of Apartments* (New York: Routledge, 2009), 59–65; and Susan Pelle and Catherine Fox, "Queering Desire/Querying Consumption: Rereading Visual Images of 'Lesbian' Desire in Lisa Cholodenko's *High Art*," *thirdspace* 6, no. 1 (2006), journals.sfu.ca/thirdspace/index.php/journal/article/view/fox-pelle/125.

8. A rare exception here is Jasbir Puar and Karen Tongson, "The Ugly Truth about Why the Kids Are All Right," *Velvetpark*, 20 January 2012, velvetparkmedia.com/blogs/ugly-truth-about-why-kids-are-all-right.

9. Justin Lowe, "*The Kids Are All Right*—Film Review," *Hollywood Reporter*, 14 October 2010, www.hollywoodreporter.com/review/kids-are-all-right-film-29203; Ella Taylor, "Talking with *The Kids Are All Right* Director Lisa Cholodenko," *Village Voice*, 29 June 2010, www.villagevoice.com/2010-06-29/film/lisa-cholodenko-s-traditional-lesbian-domestic-comedy-the-kids-are-all-right/; "*The Kids Are All Right* Resource Guide," GLAAD, www.glaad.org/kidsareallright (accessed 8 October 2011).

10. Alyssa McDonald, "Two Mums Better than One?," *Sydney Morning Herald*, 28 February 2011, www.smh.com.au/lifestyle/life/two-mums-better-than-one-20110228-1badj.html.

11. Kobena Mercer, *Welcome to the Jungle: New Positions in Black Cultural Studies* (London: Routledge, 1994), 71.

12. See, for instance, Katherine Mantle, "Our Lesbian *Brokeback*: The Kids Are All Right," *Advocate*, 8 July 2010, www.advocate.com/society/modern-families/2010/07/08/our-lesbian-brokeback-kids-are-all-right.

13. Trish Bendix, "Lisa Cholodenko on 'The Kids Are All Right,' 'High Art,' and Working on 'The L Word,'" AfterEllen, 16 November 2010, www.afterellen.com/lisa-cholodenko-on-the-kids-are-all-right-high-art-and-working-on-the-l-word/11/2010/, emphasis added.

14. Jill H. Casid, "Epilogue: Landscape In, Around, and Under the Performative," *Women and Performance* 21, no. 1 (2011): 106–7.

15. Some of these issues are also addressed in Puar and Tongson, "Ugly Truth about Why the Kids Are All Right."

16. We could also include here Moore's roles in Paul Thomas Anderson's *Boogie Nights* (US, 1997) and *Magnolia* (US, 1999).

17. For a particularly rich reading of *High Art*, see Wallace, *Lesbianism, Cinema, Space*, 59–65.

18. Production designer Julie Berghoff has said of the production design for the family's Venice home: "We wanted an Americana feeling . . . but also to suggest that they were trying to create as normal a family environment as possible." Quoted in David A. Keeps, "Set Pieces: The L.A. Look in 'The Kids Are All Right,'" *L.A. at Home* (blog), *Los Angeles Times*, 22 July 2010, latimesblogs.latimes.com/home_blog/2010/07/the-kids-are-all-rght.html.

19. Rich, "Collision, Catastrophe, Celebration," 83.

20. Claudia Gorbman, "Artless Singing," *Music, Sound, and the Moving Image* 5, no. 2 (2011): 157.

21. Barney Hoskyns, *Hotel California: The True-Life Adventures of Crosby, Stills, Nash, Young, Mitchell, Taylor, Browne, Ronstadt, Geffen, the Eagles, and Their Many Friends* (Hoboken, NJ: Wiley, 2006), 20.

22. See the chapter on *The Awful Truth* in Stanley Cavell, *Pursuits of Happiness: The Hollywood Comedy of Remarriage* (Cambridge, MA: Harvard University Press, 1981), 229–63. Cavell discusses the comedy of remarriage's transformation of festival into festivity.

Of *The Awful Truth*, he writes: "'Some grand laughs' is this comedy's lingo for marriage as festive existence" (239).

23. Few Hollywood genres have queered marriage and family as deliciously as has the comedy of remarriage with its queer parents (*The Lady Eve* [dir. Preston Sturges, US, 1941]) and its four-legged dependents (*The Awful Truth*), particularly when the genre was at its peak in the late 1930s and early 1940s. In *The Lady Eve*, Jean (Barbara Stanwyck) is a card shark who lives and travels with her father, "Colonel" Harrington (Charles Coburn), and his companion/partner Gerald (Melville Cooper). In *The Awful Truth* Lucy Warriner (Irene Dunne) and Jerry Warriner (Cary Grant) have a custody battle over their only dependent, their dog, when the couple divorces.

24. Logan Hill, "Sundance: Annette Bening and Julianne Moore Wow the Fest with a Gay Marriage Drama," Vulture, 26 January 2010, vulture.com/2010/01/sundance_annette_bening_and _ju.html.

25. A Google search for "pitch-perfect" + "the kids are all right" returns over 440,000 results and one for "note-perfect" + "the kids are all right" over 68,000, giving some indication of how limited in terrain the discussion of the film has been and how much it seems to have relied on press-package materials. The phrase *pitch perfect* has been used to describe nearly every aspect of the film—the dialogue, the actors' performances, and, more generally, the portrayal of family life. Of course, it is this pitch-perfectness that is seen as making the film's story so recognizable and so broadly appealing.

26. Burwell credits musician Marc Ribot with coming up with the film's signature guitar sound. Burwell comments: "Instrumentally the score walks a line between acoustic and electric." Carter Burwell, "*The Kids Are All Right*," The Body, www.thebodyinc.com/projects/KAAR.html (accessed 26 January 2013).

27. *The New Shorter Oxford English Dictionary*, ed. Lesley Brown (Oxford: Clarendon Press, 1993), s.v. "distort."

28. Just how precarious this space might be is exemplified by an extraordinary passage on the interior design blog *CasaSugar* on the POPSUGAR website:

The new film *The Kids Are All Right*, out in limited release today, looks intriguing; Annette Bening and Julianne Moore play a lesbian couple with Mark Ruffalo as their sperm donor. While I probably won't rush to the theater to see it, I am loving looking through photos of the film's sets. The interiors are classic, calm, sophisticated, and homey. Better yet, the look is completely attainable. It actually reminds me a lot of the house I grew up in. Want to learn how to get the look? ("Get the Look: *The Kids Are All Right*," POPSUGAR home, 9 July 2010, www.casasugar.com/Get-Look-Set-Design-From-Kids-All-Right-2010-07-09-063000-9040036)

Against the use of the present continuous for the interiors ("I am loving"), the film itself, like the lesbian occupants of those interiors, is rendered disposable, ephemeral, and dismissible.

Jodi Brooks is a senior lecturer in film studies in the School of the Arts and Media, University of New South Wales. Her essays on film time, spectatorship, and film sound have appeared in journals such as *Screen, Screening the Past,* and *Continuum* and in a number of edited collections. She is currently working on a project on performing children in film.

Figure 3. Nic and Jules. *The Kids Are All Right*

Figure 1. *Lovely and Amazing* (dir. Nicole Holofcener, US, 2001)

Beyond Indiewood: The Everyday Ethics of Nicole Holofcener

Claire Perkins

In Neil LaBute's *Your Friends and Neighbors* (US, 1998), Catherine Keener plays Terri, a starkly misanthropic figure who claims that relationships, care, and love are all a "disease." Shortly after, in Nicole Holofcener's *Lovely and Amazing* (US, 2001), Keener plays Michelle, a thirty-six-year-old who embarks on an affair with a seventeen-year-old male colleague from her job at a one-hour photo lab. In a scene toward the end of the film, the boy's mother comes across Michelle and her son making out in a car late at night. Abashed, Michelle starts to apologize to the boy's mother for how "weird" the scene looks before breaking off to comment, "That's funny—I have that same robe." In both films, Keener's characters are central to an examination of the emotional dysfunction of the white middle class. Both films use naturalistic conventions to show ordinary people in recognizable places and situations; they are prototypical indie or "Indiewood" films.[1] Beyond these broad similarities, though, the sensibilities of the two are markedly different, most notably in their relationships to gender and ethics.

In LaBute's film, Keener's trademark dry manner is channeled into a caustic persona who symbolizes the empathic bankruptcy of women of her social class. In the film's blank and symmetrical mise-en-scène, the ensemble of characters—three women and three men—stands out as a group of highly stylized types representing attitudes of cruelty, narcissism, and jealousy. In Holofcener's film, Keener's distinctive manner is mobilized in a character who is gawky and funny as well as narcissistic and snarky. Keener's distracted fixation on the mother's robe may mock middle-class values and behavior, but it does not reduce female experience to a caricature of malaise.

Building on existing critical writing on the gendering of the indie sphere,[2] this essay argues that Holofcener's oeuvre puts forward a distinct ethical position, one that is not readily absorbed or valued by the brand of commercial-independent hybridity—Indiewood—that LaBute's film signals. Given the male-driven dominant narrative of US indie cinema and particularly of the "'smart' film," it is important to restore women's contributions and perspectives.[3] Moreover, the everydayness and the ethical dimensions of the women's stories that Holofcener tells offer a sharp critique of the smart film's ironic and dissimulative pose. I use "ethics" in a sense that is broadly derived from Stanley Cavell's notion of "perfectionism," which argues that the quest for human fulfillment and self-knowledge is a moral imperative that structures film narrative. Cavell argues that this imperative is evident in an implicit line of questioning through which characters reflect on "how they shall live their lives and what kind of persons they aspire to be."[4] In the ordinary situations and character-centered drama of indie film, this reflective quest is the central point of narrative intrigue: action focuses on characters' processes of questioning, confusion, and (attempted) transformation.

Although there are numerous women directors working in the indie sector, their versions of this quest are far from the dominant narrative.[5] This is immediately clear in the work by Peter Biskind, John Pierson, Geoff King, James Mottram, and Jesse

Fox-Mayshark that collectively advances a myth of the "maverick" male auteur.[6] Figures like LaBute, Hal Hartley, and Todd Solondz craft provocative situations and relationships in a defiant refusal of mainstream conventions of narrative, style, and characterization. Seeking to understand this bias, I argue that indie discourse relies on particular gendered notions of authorship, ethics, and style. Films by female directors working in this sphere challenge this discourse and are key to understanding Indiewood despite their relative lack of prominence in accounts of its formation. For example, understanding Holofcener's contribution illuminates the work of emerging women filmmakers like Lena Dunham, one of her most visible and important successors. Dunham's work explores a similar world of class and white-skin privilege with a blunt and verbose self-awareness that is typical of this cinema's smart tone. Part of why Dunham's work has been so provocative is that it seems unprecedented, but I suggest that it builds on the work of female directors like Holofcener, whose unfussy style and frank perspective on women's desires, ambitions, and insecurities have not been as marketable as the stylized films of male directors.

Boy Wonders

Indie film is no longer strictly defined by industrial or financial contexts but is ideologically positioned more broadly in opposition to a mainstream other.[7] Signifying a taste culture that claims an artistry and legitimacy for its films and audiences over and against the commodity ethos of the multiplex, independence in the contemporary era has been co-opted by the studios in their creation or acquisition of "mini-major" operations such as Miramax (Disney, now defunct), Focus Features (Universal), Fox Searchlight, and Sony Classics. As Yannis Tzioumakis describes, this process of institutionalization has transformed US independent cinema into a type of filmmaking practiced mainly by the majors—"an 'industrial category,' much like genre and auteurism."[8] The marginalization of female directors in and through the industrial and critical discourse of US indie cinema is effected most powerfully in the maverick myth that cultivates star auteurs such as Quentin

Tarantino, Wes Anderson, and Charlie Kaufman.[9] In a manner that explicitly recalls the "gender-bound enthusiasm" of the original *politique des auteurs*,[10] these male directors are the "rebels on the backlot" who "take back Hollywood."[11] They are credited with the transformation of commercial filmmaking into a better, more artistic type of popular fare. This reception evokes the Hollywood renaissance era of 1967–75, whose male mavericks, like Arthur Penn and Terrence Malick, have been similarly cast as forging an adventurous new cinema that linked the traditions of classical genre filmmaking with the stylistic innovations of European art cinema. Both the New Hollywood and indie cycles can be characterized in the terms Andrew Sarris uses to describe the former—a cinema of "alienation, anomie, anarchy, and absurdism"[12]—for their focus on character and atmosphere over plot, their taste for violence and other taboo subject matter, and their intense self-consciousness and use of allusion and quotation.

In an update of this discourse, Jeffrey Sconce coined the term *"smart" film* in 2002 to characterize a group of films and cultural works, including *Your Friends and Neighbors*, that reviewers in the popular press had labeled "nihilistic" and "sadistic." Contextualizing the films in terms of the 1990s "irony epidemic," Sconce argues that such responses missed the strategic use of irony, which was mobilized as a way of putting the films' "offensive" content in "giant quotation marks."[13] Taking this logic further in my book on the smart film, I argue that smart cinema constitutes a contemporary movement in which films mobilize techniques of irony and blankness to position themselves knowingly in relation to film historical discourses of authorship, genre, narrative, and style. Thus directors take a dissimulative approach to their signatures or brands. As figures who are hyperconscious of auteur theory as the decipherment of a personal vision and of the way auteurism is framed by contemporary technologies and ideologies, these directors adopt a double voice. That is, they strive to evoke a sincere emotional response while simultaneously creating possibilities for the audience to see through the mechanisms that elicit that response. The result is a highly stylized and often claustrophobic look. This very marketable approach, however, discursively excludes from view the female directors who do not subscribe to this look.[14]

In the work undertaken to date on the industrial, textual, and sociocultural dimensions of this style of dissimulative authorship, critics have paid limited attention to the gendered nature of the phenomenon. This essay seeks to redress this imbalance by examining how the look of dissimulative authorship has come to brand the indie sensibility, and then considering how similar themes and tropes are expressed differently in the work of Holofcener and other female directors. This new line of inquiry constitutes an ideological approach to smart cinema, a phenomenon that I have previously characterized in primarily aesthetic terms. My objective is to understand the marginalization of women within the popular terms of this discourse and to appreciate the specific innovations female authorship has brought to independent cinema.

Exactly what constitutes female authorship is a much discussed and contested topic. One reason for the lack of critical attention to female directors in indie cinema—and in most other types of popular cinema—is a fear of what Judith Mayne has called the "dreaded epithet" of essentialism, of positing the assumption that there is a connection between a writer's gender, her personhood, and her texts.[15] In a recent survey of the "decades of embarrassed deconstruction" that have evaded the matter of female authorship, though, Catherine Grant indicates how current scholarship is operating as a kind of "reverse discourse." Women's agency, she concludes, can "finally . . . be subjected to analysis in the form of its textual, biographical traces, alongside more conventionally 'legitimate' activities for feminist cultural theorists, such as applying theories to 'primary' literary and film texts in formal 'readings.'"[16]

In this vein, I take up the case of Holofcener as a director with limited recognition in industrial, popular, and scholarly contexts. Her films, which include *Walking and Talking* (US, 1996), *Lovely and Amazing*, *Friends with Money* (US, 2006), *Please Give* (US, 2010), and *Enough Said* (US, 2013), present esteemed casts of indie stars whose verbose and self-interested characters have led her to be hailed as the "female Woody Allen."[17] In distinct contrast to Allen, though, Holofcener has continually had to fight to secure funding for scripts because, in her own evaluation, "the movies are female-centric or there's no one star or it can't be pitched in a sentence."[18] A number of articles cite the "uncommercial" nature of *Lovely and Amazing*; the film was green-lit only after Holofcener agreed to shoot on digital video, finding a budget with the digital production company Blow Up Pictures that was less than that of her previous (first) feature.[19] As she said in a 2010 interview, "I'm still shooting on low budgets, though none of my movies has lost money, and I rarely get sent anything that stars a guy or is a thriller or is seriously dramatic. And I would love the opportunity to do those things."[20]

Holofcener's experience is comparable to that of other female indie directors who run up against the boy-wonder narrative. In the discourse based on that narrative, female-directed films are seen as unclassifiable and thereby unmarketable, or are indistinctly absorbed into mainstream categories. Michele Schreiber identifies this phenomenon in her discussion of how Holofcener's films are routinely labeled "chick flicks" in the popular press. She asks: "Why is it easy for viewers to identify differences between independent and Hollywood 'men's' films, but not independent and Hollywood women's films?"[21] I shall attempt to isolate the difference of Holofcener's films from both Hollywood and the dominant indie aesthetic in terms of her treatment of a defining topic for the indie realm: the ethical conduct of the white middle class. Holofcener's films depart from the masculinist irony that has come to brand the indie sector. Although they also rely on black comedy and scenarios similar to those that are popular in the work of male directors, they frame these elements differently by foregrounding frank ethical questions on how best to live. In their engagement with a fundamental dimension of everydayness, Holofcener's films open the way to rethinking the indie realm as a gendered discourse.

Ethics and the Indie Realm

As numerous commentators have argued, the differentiation of indie from mainstream American filmmaking relies on existing perceptions of its broadly realist style of storytelling and representation. Films associated with an indie sensibility often inherit from art cinema an interest in personal stories, but they distance themselves from the formal practices of that tradition by presenting those stories in a recognizable manner. As Michael Z. Newman writes, "It is precisely this quality of ordinariness—of human life as a daily adventure just as worthy of our interest as the heightened spectacles of the megaplex—that gives . . . indie films their value in relation to studio films."[22] This distinction is frequently framed in terms of character and plot. Indie cinema's investment in realism amounts to an interest in character and certain types of characterization over a high-concept plot and visuals. The drama focuses on human behavior and interaction that, rather than supporting the narrative, *is* the narrative. In the rhetoric of indie culture, this dichotomy is posed as a specific form of resistance: the investment in character is read as an "advertisement of moral virtue" that extends to the most misanthropic of these films (94). The realist tendency of indie cinema thus functions as more than a form of textual difference; it is framed in ethical terms, as a choice to engage with human life as lived in historically and geographically specific contexts. In the films of female directors such as Holofcener, this engagement is notable because it is located in terms of female characters and emotion, and because it maintains an expressive, everyday sensibility over a highly stylized and mannerist approach.

The overarching moral schema of indie cinema is supported by the varying ways in which an engagement with life is articulated across different types of stories. Many films foreground the ethical dimension of their attention to ordinary lives by touching on known hot-button moral issues such as suicide (*The Virgin Suicides* [dir. Sofia Coppola, US, 1999]), abortion (*Palindromes* [dir. Todd Solondz, US, 2004]), pedophilia (*Happiness* [dir. Todd Solondz, US, 1998], *Life during Wartime* [dir. Todd Solondz, US, 2009]), and disability (*The Safety of Objects* [dir. Rose Troche, UK,

2001], *Storytelling* [dir. Todd Solondz, US, 2001], *In the Company of Men* [dir. Neil LaBute, Canada, 1997]). These films all derive their shock factor from extrapolating these situations in relation to recognizable and sometimes sympathetic characters. They thus provide exaggerated examples of indie films' concern with the manipulation of perspective and identification via tone. They all work at some level as what Jane Stadler calls "fables," or "narrative means of passing on ideas about how best to live life."[23] The critical reception of these films frequently emphasizes this moral function by evaluating the behavior of characters in their various situations and weighing how such behavior confronts audiences with their own attitudes and priorities concerning life events such as aging parents (*The Savages* [dir. Tamara Jenkins, US, 2007]), infidelity (*Your Friends and Neighbors*), divorce (*The Squid and the Whale* [dir. Noah Baumbach, US, 2005]), and same-sex marriage (*The Kids Are All Right* [dir. Lisa Cholodenko, US, 2010]). In examples like these, characters are often weighed down by self-assumed expectations about how best to manage themselves and others. In *The Savages*, for instance, Wendy (Laura Linney) describes herself and her brother, Jon (Philip Seymour Hoffman), as "terrible, terrible people" for moving their demented father into a sterile Buffalo nursing home when they should have tried for a fancier and more lushly marketed option in Vermont. In the wake of his separation in *The Squid and the Whale*, Bernard (Jeff Daniels) advises his teenage son Walt (Jesse Eisenberg) to break up with his girlfriend, suggesting that he should be "playing the field" at his age. "Should" is a word frequently uttered by indie characters.

In these scenarios, the drama arises from human interactions centered on the concept of the social self. Identity and morality are governed by observation and connection, by the ability of humans to respond to one another in their contingent circumstances rather than through abstract principles of right and good (17). Aligning with the broadly realist style of storytelling discussed above, many indie films by both male and female directors reflect this ethical principle in their narrative structures, in which a fast-moving series of short scenes weaves together episodes from various characters' lives. Rather than being presented in a linear and causal manner, stories are constantly interrupted, with intrigue arising from contrasting and parallel construction. As I have argued elsewhere, the narratives of indie cinema in this way promote an anticausal conception of life as an unpredictable and continuous series of events that palpably extend beyond the narrative.[24] In this schema, character transformation is not a singular function in a tightly plotted three-act scenario but a constant and circular process of adapting to the expectations raised by other people and everyday events. From an ethical perspective, characters are not the fixed moral agents of virtue theory—which examines how an assured self attends to others—but subjects in a state of flux.[25] In the context of the highly self-aware and intertextual character of much indie cinema, we can call these subjects discursive—subjects constructed in and through the ideas and values that a specific social environment holds on how best to live.

In most indie stories, this discursive mode of subjectivity is expressed in processes of questioning, confusion, and (attempted) transformation. Frequently couched in gendered scenarios of marriage, divorce, and infidelity, the expectations that characters impose on themselves and others—the *should* imperative—are framed by the desire for a different kind of life. In the hands of the male maverick directors, this mode of subjectivity is presented in a manner that is highly stylized and/or cynical. Everyday dramas of human interaction and aspiration are rendered contrived and quirky—simultaneously heightened and ordinary, ironic and sincere, absurd and moving, artificial and believable. Characters are not real but rather wholly plastic in the sense that their gestures and actions are created through cinema as art, not through its capacity to record real life. This is a powerful way in which smart films call to mind figures and attitudes from literature, film, television, philosophy, and popular culture. It is particularly visible in female character types: from the whimsical depressives of Anderson and Terry Zwigoff to the monstrous suburban housewives of Solondz and LaBute, from the surreal dreamers of Kaufman and Spike Jonze to the Socratic figures of Whit Stillman and Hartley. These characters are unapologetically objectified, but in ways that ironize their presentation. In other words, the content is sexist but overtly constructed, reflexive, and coded in the highly marketable terms of "quirk."

As James Macdowell writes, the quirky effect—often played for comedy—derives from a tradition of deadpan that works by incongruity, "juxtaposing histrionic subject matter with dampened execution, draining expected emotions from the potentially melodramatic."[26] While this strategy could plausibly be expected to promote an everyday mode of realism, quirky films create the exact opposite: they find significance—drama—in the force of their blank visual patterning and composition.[27] The presentation of loosely plotted episodes in this highly controlled style gives rise to the impression of tense, autonomous worlds that exist outside everyday time. Within these worlds, characters' speculation about how best to live rehearses existing attitudes rather than seeking new ones in any meaningful way. Airless environments offer no scope for reaching self-knowledge, instead sketching what I call limit situations: states of affairs in which genuine transformation is impossible for the films' narcissistic characters. As an effect focused on the quirky and dysfunctional female types outlined above, the limit situation of male maverick indie cinema offers a scathing critique of the ethical potential of the white middle class. The next section will examine the very different way in which Holofcener handles this ethical question through similar themes.

Everyday Ethics

Holofcener's films make explicit the ethical questions that, I have argued, concern indie cinema generally. In her films, though, the desire for transformation and a better way of life is manifested in the ways in which characters express and perform attitudes of care. The constant, implicit question of how to relate to others is framed by specific situations: a best friend marrying (*Walking and Talking*), a middle-aged white woman adopting a young African American girl (*Lovely and Amazing*), a wealthy couple deliberating over where to donate money (*Friends with Money*). The question is summed up in Holofcener's best-known scene in *Lovely and Amazing*, in which the character of Elizabeth (Emily Mortimer) demands and receives an honest appraisal of her naked body from a partner (Dermot Mulroney). In *Friends with Money* and *Please Give*, the broader ethical concerns of smart cinema are channeled into characters and situations dealing specifically with wealth and its impact on relationships and self-identity. *Friends with Money* concerns a group of four female friends, three who are wealthy and married and one who is poor and single, while *Please Give* focuses on the escalating guilt of its main character, Kate (Catherine Keener), over her middle-class lifestyle.

Reviewers cite Holofcener's "unsparing" but also "generous" and "profound" approach to female protagonists to claim that her films are honest about the complexity of female desire and neuroses.[28] Specifically, the idea that she presents live and grown-up women is discussed in connection with the unvarnished look of her films, in which characters are frequently depicted without makeup or with dirty hair or visible wrinkles. While these claims are often hyperbolic, they do indicate the connection of the work to the ordinary and the everyday. *Friends with Money* and *Please Give* both specifically dramatize the everydayness of marriage, dwelling on the repetitions and dissatisfactions that arise from the decision to live with one person. The routines of marriage—going to bed and waking up together, looking after children, preparing food, driving—are avoided in quirky, male-directed melodramas such as *500 Days of Summer* (dir. Marc Webb, US, 2009), *Margot at the Wedding* (dir. Noah Baumbach, US, 2007), *Rachel Getting Married* (dir. Jonathan Demme, US, 2008), *Your Friends and Neighbors*, and *The Squid and the Whale* in favor of a focus on the vivid relationship event: falling in love, getting married, having an affair, breaking up. Though marriage remains an important touchstone for the ways in which such films dramatize and ironize ordinary emotion, it is frequently a plot point of dramatic significance that supports a whimsical, taboo, or absurd agenda: for instance, the long-estranged Tenenbaum parents of *The Royal Tenenbaums* (dir. Wes Anderson, US, 2001), the secretly pedophilic husband of *Happiness*, or the surreal, escapist adventures of the staid married couple of *Being John Malkovich* (dir. Spike Jonze, US, 1999).

Holofcener's films, in contrast, present the work by which

marriage is ratified—by which couples learn to live with and acknowledge the repetitions of the everyday. In *Please Give*, this process takes the form of Kate and Alex (Oliver Platt) interacting at home and work over the shared parts of their lives: their teenage daughter, Abby (Sarah Steele), the vintage furniture they buy from deceased's estates to sell in their fashionable Tenth Avenue shop, and their elderly neighbor Andra (Ann Morgan Guilbert), whose apartment they plan to expand into once she dies. In contrast to the overwrought exchanges of other indie couples, where compositional formality often signifies personal distance, these characters are presented in a highly naturalistic manner. In one scene that follows an awkward dinner party with Andra and her granddaughters, Kate and Alex talk in their bathroom. As Alex flosses his teeth, Kate sits on the edge of the bathtub and they discuss how "awful" Andra is, confessing that her bluntness makes them feel less guilty about wanting her to die. The bathroom is white and green, with bad lighting and ordinary clutter—a towel flung over the shower railing, toiletries clustered on the sink. The scene alternates between close-ups of the two speaking and long shots of Kate and Alex reflected together in the mirror above the sink. Like many of the couple's scenes together, this conversation gestures toward Kate's insecurity over herself and her aging body, as she chides Alex for flirting with Andra's granddaughter Mary (Amanda Peet). He breezily acknowledges the flirtation, but claims he has "no idea why . . . she's such a bitch." As the germ that will develop into his short-lived affair with Mary, Alex's flirtation and Kate's response here are radically underplayed. The prevailing impression is of their attunement as a couple as they rehearse long-held attitudes, private jokes, and everyday rituals. The symbolism of their contained reflection in the mirror is powerful.

Figure 2. *Please Give* (dir. Nicole Holofcener, US, 2010)

In another scene the couple visits a local pharmacy, taking along a shopping list for Andra. As Kate looks around she happens upon Abby browsing a wall of products. She calls Alex over and the two hang back out of sight at the end of the aisle, silently and complicitly watching their daughter. The viewer's anticipation that Abby will see them, or shoplift, is overwhelming. Instead, nothing develops—the parents merely observe in muted wonder this fundamentally shared aspect of their lives. The moment is sublime, but completely unmannered in style. It lacks the intensity of the quirky moments in indie cinema by its fleeting temporality and by keeping all three characters in slightly unsteady medium or long shots. In its unemphatic and peripheral nature, the scene registers as what Andrew Klevan terms "undramatic achievement." It works via implication, "revealing what is important but hidden only because it is always—every day—before our eyes."[29] This type of revelation demonstrates the capacity of cinema to connect with the world by disclosing everydayness rather than transforming or avoiding it.

The pharmacy scene showcases Holofcener's unique everyday sensibility by resonating with the undramatic presentation of bigger events and stories in *Please Give*, especially the key theme of death. All the story lines concerning death—the eventual demise of Andra, the revelation that Mary's mother committed suicide, the deaths of the people owning the furniture that Kate and Alex buy—are disclosed in a way that downplays the status of the event itself, emphasizing instead the process of dying as something that is every day "before our eyes." The sentiment is best expressed when another elderly female character is diagnosed with cancer and claims that it's "OK" because she's old: "It's a tragedy when it happens to someone young." In another example of undramatic presentation, Alex's affair with Mary is rendered in a very mechanical way; the two appear completely disconnected from each other and their present circumstances. The affair is Alex's half-hearted attempt to escape the repetitions of everyday life with Kate where, in his weary description, they are partners—"partners at work, partners as parents, partners in life." After the second time Alex and Mary sleep together, though, Alex apologizes for starting something, and Mary says she does not want to do it anymore. The event falls flat, and Alex returns to the attuned, if uneven, rhythm of his marriage without revealing to anyone what happened.

This narrative thread is interesting for its place in the film's overall ethical agenda. *Please Give* channels the general indie concern with how to live into the specific problem of how to relate to others as a member of the relatively affluent white middle class. Thus, Alex's conduct in his affair is set alongside the action he undertakes with Kate—buying Andra's apartment to expand into and making a substantial profit with their furniture business. In each case the action is staged as an ethical question insofar as it becomes a point of contention between characters. When, in bed, Mary voices the cliché that people only have affairs when there is something missing in the marriage, Alex retorts that some say an affair can help a marriage and, in an expression of genuine hope, that maybe this one will help his. In a broader way, the fundamental conflict between Kate's and Alex's worldviews is mobilized to express the problems and dissatisfactions of the everyday experience of marriage. Unlike Alex's character, Kate's is explicitly defined by liberal guilt. She firmly believes that her own good fortune comes with the responsibility of feeling bad for those who are homeless, elderly, or disabled. She defensively obscures the facts of the couple's work that Alex comfortably acknowledges, and feels compelled to abide by values of moderation to justify her own comfort. "I am not spending two-hundred dollars on a pair of jeans for my teenage daughter when there are forty-five homeless people living on our street," she tells Abby. Her guilt, Alex says, is "warping" both of them; it is after an exchange in the shop about how he is "OK" with what they do that he first visits Mary.

Such disagreements over recognizable ethical issues form part of a broader pattern in *Please Give*, where character interaction is structured around the clashing of fixed ideas on what promotes happiness, health, and morality. People implore one another to travel upstate to see the beautiful spectacle of the autumn leaves changing color. Kate laments that Andra cannot leave her apartment to go outside and see the world. Mary's sister Rebecca (Rebecca Hall) criticizes Mary for behavior that is "bad for her": tanning, microwaving, drinking, spying on her ex's new girlfriend. An unnamed man Rebecca meets for a date claims that New York is filthy and crime-ridden—a terrible place to raise children. Andra says that no one told the building superintendent—whom Kate pities for being poor—to have so many children. Abby tells a woman in a clothing shop that she should not charge so much for jeans. Mary argues that people should be honest: "If you get a sucky haircut people should admit it."

As attitudes that are directly or implicitly challenged when expressed, such positions present individual perspectives on the best way to live as giving rise to funny and uncomfortable encounters. The restlessness that belies a desire for change is cast in blackly comic terms, with characters sniping at each other's "stupid" beliefs and values. While most of these desires are presented as narcissistic, Kate's are social. Her perspective entails striving for a self that is better in the world, a self that gives money, time, and empathy. When she inquires about volunteering at a nursing home she is asked what makes her think this is a good time in her life to do so. Kate responds that "something" is telling her to do more—that giving money is easy, but that she wants to "give something, to someone." The crushing but nonspecific nature of this drive to give—her liberal guilt—is forcefully demonstrated when she is taken to meet some of the residents and, against the airy advice of the manager to keep her manner upbeat and positive, voices her shock at how "bent over" a woman with rheumatoid arthritis is. The scenario is amplified in a later scene where she visits a group of disabled teenagers playing basketball and, after being introduced to a girl named Abby, is ushered out crying. Within the context of the film's overall agenda, the scenes are compelling for the ways in which they stage the dilemma of complicity.

In posing contrasts between broadly drawn attitudes of those who give (Kate and Rebecca) and those who take (Mary, Abby, Andra), *Please Give* asks its spectators (educated, middle-class fans of indie cinema) to confront their collusion in both narcissistic desire and guilt and self-sacrifice. The film, however, complicates the conventional morality of these positions by aligning them with different worldviews: where Kate perceives suffering and hopelessness in everything before her—such as the homeless, the elderly, the disabled, and the exploitative logic of capitalism—others see the norms and repetitions of everyday life. One of the teens playing basketball encourages Kate to have a shot at the hoop, reassuring her that "you try, you fail, you try again." In this situation, Kate is positioned as the unethical figure, embarrassing herself and the caregiver by crying in front of the teens and apologizing profusely. The scene shows that her guilt does not make her better but rather is part of the confusion of desires that she, and everyone, struggles with in yearning to connect with the world in a more meaningful way.

Holofcener's staging of ethical implication differs radically from the limit situation in the films of the male directors discussed above. LaBute, Baumbach, and Stillman show the white middle class as unable to care for others or achieve self-knowledge. The empty malaise of this message is often carried by female characters who are presented as unethical, uncaring, and unintuitive. Margot (Nicole Kidman) in Baumbach's *Margot at the Wedding* amplifies the stance of judgment that defines all indie characters into a monstrous portrayal of a flailing, destructive mother and sister. As a figure written in overtly intellectual terms—as many smart film characters are—Margot, a writer, expresses her own unhappiness and anger by criticizing and demoralizing her sister, son, and husband for not being sufficiently ambitious or complex in their life choices. The ugliness of her character appears in a different mode in the collective of archaic college girls in Stillman's comedy of sexual politics, *Damsels in Distress* (US, 2011). Here, the character of Violet (Greta Gerwig) leads a campus self-help program that seeks to improve the social manners and well-being of students—in short, to teach them to live better. With crass frat boys as a target, the girls are presented as smugly self-possessed saints who dispense advice in formal etiquette and propose that happiness exists in the minor therapies of doughnuts and tap dancing. The ethical codes of the white middle class are reduced to quirky caricatures, which the moralizing girls impart in a zealous and self-serving mission that knowingly overrides any actual potential for care. In the emphatic self-reflexivity of these films, the mannerist mark of the director is felt as a form of judgment.

The plastic and ironic figures and situations highlight spectatorship as a practice of recognition and interpretation by which the spectator gets—or fails to get—the film's stark viewpoint. Moreover, the spectator is positioned not only to judge the flattened characters but also to recognize his or her reflection in them. The most critical dimension of the film's uncompromising or nihilistic perspective lies in the proposition that the spectator is complicit in perpetuating the world that is shown.

In contrast to the highly commentative style of expression in such films by male directors, the mode of disclosure that characterizes Holofcener's work functions expressively. As Holofcener has claimed, "I want the look of the movie to be secondary. I really want people to be engaged in the story and the characters and not think about a style or think about me or think about the D.P. and what a great job he's doing. I never feel like that should be there."[30] Consequently, significance does not enter the shot by way of a nondiegetic agenda but rather issues from the action and characters. Holofcener openly describes how the situations that ground her films are derived from her own life: her mother's adoption late in life of a young African American girl, her feelings about her best friend's engagement, her fascination with vintage furniture shops in New York. As the director's alter ego, Keener is an important figure. According to Holofcener, the actress "is more myself in these movies than she is herself."[31] Specifically, Keener stands for Holofcener's embarrassment at a materialist, image-bound world and her place within it. But, in a step to the side of the self-reflexivity and judgment that pervade the indie sector, this alter ego provides Holofcener with a way of, in her terms, "laughing at herself"—at the fact she likes "nice stuff" but ultimately sees the futility of it. Her acknowledgment of the predictability and faint absurdity of her own middle-class behavior gives rise to her critique of the tropes and clichés that shape "dishonest" Hollywood films about women.[32] This self-effacing position stands in stark contrast to the arch, dissimulative approach of the male directors of other commercial-independent films, whose authorial presence becomes an ironic gesture embedded in both the work and its promotion.

The everyday register of Holofcener's work positions it

against the narcissistic limit situation of so many indie films. Characters' restlessness, confusion, and humiliation are not depicted in terms of quiet, urgent hysteria or breakdown—as, for example, in *Amateur* (dir. Hal Hartley, US, 1994) or *Safe* (dir. Todd Haynes, US, 1995)—but are dramatized in the simple refusal to constrain characters to one archetypal perspective. Ultimately, this lack of constraint enables a different perspective on the possibility of human transformation. In all of Holofcener's films, Keener's character is central to this effect. Amelia in *Walking and Talking* is at once mortified and reflective upon being caught calling a date "the ugly guy." Michelle in *Lovely and Amazing* suggests to her adopted sister that she might have inherited genes that make her "better" than the rest of the family. Christine in *Friends with Money* becomes wracked with guilt and shame when she realizes that the enormous extension she and her husband are building will obscure their neighbors' view. In direct opposition to the resolutely selfish figures Keener plays in *Your Friends and Neighbors*, *Being John Malkovich*, and *Synecdoche, New York* (dir. Charlie Kaufman, US, 2008), Keener under Holofcener's direction epitomizes the way in which so many of Holofcener's characters step back and regard their situations, becoming aware of how their behavior affects others. In each of Holofcener's films, action breaks the limit situation to achieve a small measure of modulation, though without any guarantee of permanence: in *Please Give*, Rebecca does travel upstate to see the leaves, Mary steps in to shop for Andra, and—in the film's final scene—Kate buys Abby her two-hundred-dollar jeans. As one reviewer describes it, "All of Holofcener's movies have this moment when self-involvement bordering on narcissism is disturbed and then broken like the yolk of an egg."[33]

Conclusion

Holofcener's ability to break what I have called the limit situation of the dominant indie ethic and aesthetic is echoed in the work of other female directors of smart US indie films—figures like Dunham, Tamara Jenkins, Sarah Polley, Lynn Shelton, and Jennifer Westfeldt. Dunham's concern with female experience and how to live, and her direct but clever style, especially resonate with Holofcener's. Dunham is also susceptible to the "chick flick" label insofar as she frames traditionally feminine content—relationships and female friendships—in the funny and uncomfortable terms of everyday experience. With this approach, her work—like Holofcener's—is caught between realms: it is not readily classifiable in terms of mainstream Hollywood, the quirky indie sector, or the style of social realism that is more popularly associated with a feminist agenda (in, for instance, the films of Kelly Reichardt, Courtney Hunt, or Debra Granik).

Dunham's forthright comedies of female experience—the feature film *Tiny Furniture* (US, 2010) and HBO series *Girls* (2012–)—emphasize the potential for character modulation. Their protagonists (both played by Dunham) are serious and engaged but also deeply funny in their pursuit of a full and authentic existence. With its connection to the "mumblecore" movement, Dunham's work promotes the authenticity of both talk and action through her low-key and realistic approach to staging and style. As in Holofcener's films, meaning issues from Dunham's (also autobiographical) characters and action rather than from a contrived and ironic style. The sensibility is blunt but does not broach the dissimulative terms of deadpan.

Restoring Holofcener's place within the smart tradition of indie cinema helps to explain the emergence of Dunham's filmmaking. Like most indie cinema, the work of both these female directors functions in an observational mode, attending to loosely plotted episodes of ordinary life. The films hold a unique identity within the realm of smart cinema due to their use of a tonal register that is simultaneously snarky and real and a specific sensitivity to ethical questions of everyday female existence. This essay has suggested that these qualities demonstrate how Holofcener's work transforms, and thus affords a new perspective on, the masculinist, ironic mode of expression that brands the indie discourse. Holofcener's characters are offbeat but not archetypes; their moral conflicts cannot be shut down with whimsical or nihilistic endings; and their self-awareness is never mobilized as a posture that overwhelms the frank concerns of the films themselves. Rather than transforming habitual confusions and dissatisfactions into abstract terms or transcending them, her films acknowledge and stay with everydayness, channeling characters' confused desires into shifting patterns of identification and empathy. By locating intrigue in small-scale action and not large expression, Holofcener is an ethical figure in the indie sector: she and her characters acknowledge the moral cynicism of a fixed perspective on life and thus connect with the world in a different way. In this sense, her films are an important example of how indie women's filmmaking can change the traditions, paradigms, and institutions in which it is embedded.

Notes

1. The Indiewood realm is discussed in Geoff King, *Indiewood, USA: Where Hollywood Meets Independent Cinema* (London: I. B. Tauris, 2009).

2. See especially Christina Lane, *Feminist Hollywood: From "Born in Flames" to "Point Break"* (Detroit: Wayne State University Press, 2000); and Christina Lane, "Just Another Girl Outside the Neo-Indie," in *Contemporary American Independent Film: From the Margins to the Mainstream*, ed. Chris Holmlund and Justin Wyatt (New York: Routledge, 2005), 193–209.

3. Jeffrey Sconce, "Irony, Nihilism, and the New American 'Smart' Film," *Screen* 43, no. 4 (2002): 349–69.

4. Stanley Cavell, *Cities of Words: Pedagogical Letters on a Register of the Moral Life* (Cambridge, MA: Belknap Press of Harvard University Press, 2004), 11.

5. Lane attends to the figures of Allison Anders, Julie Dash, Leslie Harris, Lynn Hershman Leeson, Nancy Savoca, and Rose Troche. Other writers and directors who showcase recognizable themes and players in their work and participate regularly in indie institutions such as the Sundance Film Festival and the Independent Spirit Awards include Lisa Cholodenko, Lena Dunham, Debra Granik, Courtney Hunt, Tamara Jenkins, Miranda July, So Young Kim, Karyn Kusama, Karen Moncrieff, Kimberly Peirce, Sarah Polley, Kelly Reichardt, Adrienne Shelley, Lynn Shelton, and Jennifer Westfeldt.

6. Peter Biskind, *Down and Dirty Pictures: Miramax, Sundance, and the Rise of Independent Film* (New York: Simon & Schuster, 2004); John Pierson, *Spike, Mike, Slackers, and Dykes: A Guided Tour across a Decade of American Independent Cinema* (New York: Miramax/Hyperion, 1995); Geoff King, *American Independent Cinema* (New York: I. B. Tauris, 2005); King, *Indiewood, USA*; Geoff King, *Indie 2.0: Change and Continuity in Contemporary American Indie Film* (New York: I. B. Tauris, 2013); James Mottram, *The Sundance Kids: How the Mavericks Took Back Hollywood* (London: Faber and Faber, 2006); Jesse Fox-Mayshark, *Post-Pop Cinema: The Search for Meaning in New American Film* (Westport, CT: Praeger, 2007).

7. Michael Z. Newman, *Indie: An American Film Culture* (New York: Columbia University Press, 2011).

8. Yannis Tzioumakis, *American Independent Cinema: An Introduction* (Edinburgh: Edinburgh University Press, 2006), 247.

9. See, for instance, Mottram, *Sundance Kids*.

10. Angela Martin, "Refocusing Authorship in Women's Filmmaking," in *Women Filmmakers: Refocusing*, ed. Jacqueline Levitin, Judith Plessis, and Valerie Raoul (New York: Routledge, 2003), 31.

11. Sharon Waxman, *Rebels on the Backlot: Six Maverick Directors and How They Conquered the Hollywood Studio System* (New York: Harper Perennial, 2006); Mottram, *Sundance Kids*.

12. Andrew Sarris, "After *The Graduate*," *American Film* 3, no. 9 (1978): 37.

13. Sconce, "New American 'Smart' Film," 358.

14. See Claire Perkins, *American Smart Cinema* (Edinburgh: Edinburgh University Press, 2012), esp. 27–28.

15. Judith Mayne, *The Woman at the Keyhole: Feminism and Women's Cinema* (Bloomington: Indiana University Press, 1990), 90.

16. Catherine Grant, "Secret Agents: Feminist Theories of Women's Film Authorship," *Feminist Theory* 2, no. 1 (2001): 123.

17. Most articles on Holofcener cite her family connection to Allen. When she was eight, her mother married Charles Joffe, who, until his death in 2008, coproduced all of Allen's films. Holofcener was an extra in Allen's *Take the Money and Run* (US,

1969) and *Sleeper* (US, 1973) and later worked as a production assistant on other films of his. See Christine Spines, "Pursuits of Happiness," *Film Comment* 46, no. 2 (2010): 34–38.

18. Steve Erickson, "The Lovely and Amazing Nicole Holofcener," *Los Angeles Magazine*, 1 May 2010, www.lamag.com/features/2010/05/01/the-lovely-and-amazing-nicole-holofcener.

19. Patricia Thomson, "Femme Helmers Strive for Level Playing Field," *Variety*, 28 July 2002, variety.com/2002/scene/markets-festivals/femme-helmers-strive-for-level-playing-field-1117870380/.

20. Erickson, "Lovely and Amazing Nicole Holofcener."

21. Michele Schreiber, "Independence at What Cost? Economics and Female Desire in Nicole Holofcener's *Friends with Money* (2006)," in *Feminism at the Movies: Understanding Gender in Contemporary Popular Cinema*, ed. Hilary Radner and Rebecca Stringer (New York: Routledge, 2011), 180.

22. Newman, *Indie*, 88–89.

23. Jane Stadler, *Pulling Focus: Intersubjective Experience, Narrative Film, and Ethics* (New York: Continuum, 2008), 19.

24. See Perkins, *American Smart Cinema*, 58–73.

25. Joseph Kupfer uses the framework of virtue theory to discuss *Friends with Money* in Joseph Kupfer, *Feminist Ethics in Film: Reconfiguring Care through Cinema* (Bristol, UK: Intellect, 2012).

26. James Macdowell, "Notes on Quirky," *Movie*, no. 1 (2010), www2.warwick.ac.uk/fac/arts/film/movie/contents/notes_on_quirky.pdf.

27. The effect can be likened to the "melodrama of time" that Andrew Klevan describes in his Cavell-influenced work. Here, neorealist depictions of ordinary life such as those favored by Gilles Deleuze in his conception of the time-image are pushed to their limits by time, which "appears to be pressing in the shot, stretched, and tense." Andrew Klevan, *Disclosure of the Everyday: Undramatic Achievement in Narrative Film* (Trowbridge, UK: Flicks Books, 2000), 46.

28. Spines, "Pursuits of Happiness," 35; Erickson, "Lovely and Amazing Nicole Holofcener."

29. Klevan, *Disclosure of the Everyday*, 30.

30. Nicole Holofcener, interview by Scott Tobias, *A.V. Club*, 29 April 2010, www.avclub.com/articles/nicole-holofcener,40605/.

31. Holofcener, interview by Scott Tobias.

32. Spines, "Pursuits of Happiness," 35.

33. Erickson, "Lovely and Amazing Nicole Holofcener."

Claire Perkins is a lecturer in film and television studies at Monash University. She is the author of *American Smart Cinema* (Edinburgh University Press, 2012) and coeditor of *Film Trilogies: New Critical Approaches* (Palgrave Macmillan, 2012) and *B Is for Bad Cinema: Aesthetics, Politics, and Cultural Value* (SUNY Press, 2014).

Figure 3. *Please Give*

THE OHIO STATE UNIVERSITY PRESS
ohiostatepress.org - 800-621-2736

THE READER AS PEEPING TOM
Nonreciprocal Gazing in Narrative Fiction and Film

Jeremy Hawthorn

$69.95 cloth 978-0-8142-1257-8
$14.95 CD 978-0-8142-9360-7

Theory and Interpretation of Narrative - Series Editors
James Phelan, Peter J. Rabinowitz, and Robyn Warhol